Surveillance and the Law

T0386315

Surveillance of citizens is a clear manifestation of government power. The act of surveillance is generally deemed acceptable in a democratic society where it is necessary to protect the interests of the nation and where the power is exercised non-arbitrarily and in accordance with the law.

Surveillance and the Law: Language, Power, and Privacy analyses the core features of surveillance that create stark challenges for transparency and accountability by examining the relationship between language, power, and surveillance. It identifies a number of features of surveillance law, surveillance language, and the distribution of power that perpetuate the existing surveillance paradigm. Using case studies from the US, the UK, and Ireland, it assesses the techniques used to maintain the status quo of continued surveillance expansion. These jurisdictions are selected for their similarities, but also for their key constitutional distinctions, which influence how power is distributed and restrained in the different systems. Though the book maintains that the classic principles of transparency and accountability remain the best means available to limit the arbitrary exercise of government power, it evaluates how these principles could be better realised in order to restore power to the people and to maintain an appropriate balance between government intrusion and the right to privacy.

By identifying the common tactics used in the expansion of surveillance around the globe, this book will appeal to students and scholars interested in privacy law, human rights, information technology law, and surveillance studies.

Maria Helen Murphy is a lecturer in law at Maynooth University, Ireland.

Surveillance and the Law
Language, Power, and Privacy

Maria Helen Murphy

Routledge
Taylor & Francis Group

LONDON AND NEW YORK

First published 2019 by Routledge

2 Park Square, Milton Park, Abingdon, Oxfordshire OX14 4RN

52 Vanderbilt Avenue, New York, NY 10017

Routledge is an imprint of the Taylor & Francis Group, an informa business

First issued in paperback 2020

British Library Cataloguing-in-Publication Data
A catalogue record for this book is available from the British Library

Library of Congress Cataloging-in-Publication Data
A catalog record for this book has been requested

ISBN: 978-1-138-59990-1 (hbk)
ISBN: 978-0-367-60672-5 (pbk)

Typeset in Times New Roman
by Apex CoVantage, LLC

Contents

Acknowledgements

I would first like to thank all of my colleagues and students at Maynooth University for continuing to provide a stimulating and collegial work environment. Thanks also to Emer Shannon, Jack Murphy, and Ger Maguire for their last-minute assistance. I am grateful to everyone at Routledge who worked on this book, especially to Siobhán Poole. I am also very appreciative of the invaluable efforts of colleagues – in academia and beyond – working in the areas of privacy and surveillance. Finally, I would like to thank David and the rest of my family for their constant support.

Introduction

The most prominent piece of literature on the power of the surveillance state – George Orwell's 1984 – identifies the use and manipulation of language as a key element of government control. There is a case to be made that 'Big Brother's most potent tool for policing society had little to do with controlling computers, and everything to do with controlling truth'.[1] The language around surveillance has often been the subject of 'semantic facelifting' where those in power have euphemistically described their surveillance activities. Consider the shift from 'bugging' to 'electronic surveillance', 'wiretapping' to 'highly confidential coverage', and 'asset' to 'informer'.[2] More recently, states resist the use of the term 'mass surveillance' in favour of 'bulk collection' and governments no longer 'spy', they simply engage in 'data collection'.[3] Obscuring truth from the citizen conflicts with the most basic conceptions of democracy which rest on 'some sense that people are able to think and make judgements for themselves'.[4] It should be remembered

1 Brett Kaufman, 'Dragnet surveillance and the English language' (2014) 33(4) *The Washington Report on Middle East Affairs* 9.
2 Frank Donner, *The Age of Surveillance: The Aims and Methods of America's Political Intelligence System* (Vintage Books 1980) 464.
3 Zygmunt Bauman, Didier Bigo, Paulo Esteves, Elspeth Guild, Vivienne Jabri, David Lyon, and Rob Walker, 'After Snowden: Rethinking the Impact of Surveillance' (2014) 8 *International Political Sociology* 121, 143; Glen Greenwald, 'The Orwellian Re-Branding of "Mass Surveillance" as Merely "Bulk Collection"' (*The Intercept*, 13 March 2015) <https://theintercept.com/2015/03/13/orwellian-re-branding-mass-surveillance-merely-bulk-collection/>
4 Zygmunt Bauman, Didier Bigo, Paulo Esteves, Elspeth Guild, Vivienne Jabri, David Lyon, and Rob Walker, 'After Snowden: Rethinking the Impact of Surveillance' (2014) 8 *International Political Sociology* 121, 143; Miguelángel Verde Garrido, 'Contesting a Biopolitics of Information and Communications: The Importance of Truth and Sousveillance After Snowden' (2015) 13(2) *Surveillance & Society* 153, 162.

that governance itself is a form of control 'in that it aims to steer and direct individuals, encouraging them to embrace particular behaviours'.[5] Such efforts at social control are not inherently negative in a democratic society, but measures must be in place to prevent arbitrary and disproportionate control. In the surveillance context, constitutional and human rights documents have an important role to play as surveillance measures will tend to have profound implications for the protection of the right to privacy and, indeed, the protection of free expression. While the surveillance of citizens is a clear manifestation of government power, constitutional and human rights documents are designed to limit the arbitrary exercise of that power.

Differences of opinion regarding the 'correct' interpretation of language frequently arise in law. When language is manipulated or interpreted in a way that circumvents or limits rights and freedoms, serious issues arise. The ambiguity of human language limits the precision of all law, but the secrecy prevalent in the surveillance sphere magnifies the effect. The problem of limiting rights and freedoms is exacerbated where they are restricted in a covert manner resulting in citizens being denied the opportunity to protest or demand recalibration. While much of what makes the relationship between language and power in the surveillance context worthy of specific inquiry rests on the secrecy that surrounds surveillance measures, an additional factor that cannot be underestimated is the technical nature of the subject matter. Technical language – prevalent in the field of surveillance – has an obfuscatory effect that can restrict understanding to a limited group of privileged insiders and experts. Changes in the structures of communications technology have also transformed the meanings of key terms that have previously been used to demarcate appropriate action. One of the most noted examples of this is how the meaning of what is 'foreign' and what is 'domestic' has become blurred as a result of the modern globalised communications infrastructure.[6]

This book draws from examples from the United States, the United Kingdom and Ireland in order to examine the relationship between

---

5 Kevin Haggerty, 'Foreword' in Sean Hier and Josh Greenberg (eds), *Surveillance: Power, Problems, and Politics* (UBC Press 2009) xvii.
6 Zygmunt Bauman, Didier Bigo, Paulo Esteves, Elspeth Guild, Vivienne Jabri, David Lyon, and Rob Walker, 'After Snowden: Rethinking the Impact of Surveillance' (2014) 8 *International Political Sociology* 121, 128. This distinction is traditionally considered important for national security purposes, although the following words of James Madison suggest the prudence of scepticism: 'Perhaps it is a universal truth that the loss of liberty at home is to be charged to provisions against danger, real or pretended, from abroad'. James Madison to Thomas Jefferson (13 May 1798) as cited in Walter LaFeber, 'The Constitution and United States Foreign Policy: An Interpretation' (1987) 74(3) *The Journal of American History* 695, 697.

language, power, privacy, and surveillance. As a preliminary matter, examining the relationship between language and power in each of these jurisdictions requires an understanding of their constitutional structures.[7] To varying degrees, a separation of powers between the branches of the executive, legislative, and judicial applies in each jurisdiction. As acknowledged by James Madison in *The Federalist* Papers, 'the accumulation of all powers, legislative, executive, and judiciary, in the same hands, whether of one, a few, or many, and whether hereditary, self-appointed, or elective, may justly be pronounced the very definition of tyranny'.[8] In a system of constitutional democracy, where personal liberties were to be protected, the framers of the US Constitution believed it necessary to ensure that no individual or entity would 'be blindly trusted to wield power wisely'.[9] The separation of powers principle – or the concept of 'separated institutions, shared powers' – is designed to prevent misuse of power by ensuring it is not concentrated in a particular branch.[10]

In both the UK and Ireland, the executive branch and the legislative branch are fused; with the heads of the respective executives – the Prime Minister and the Taoiseach – being the leaders of the majority parties in Parliament and the Oireachtas respectively.[11] The fact that a strong whip tradition exists in both jurisdictions further reinforces the fusion of power between the national parliaments and the executive branches. As a result, there is little legislative constraint on executive action. In addition to having written constitutions,[12] both the US and Ireland have strong traditions

7 In the Irish constitutional context, see *Bunreacht na hÉireann* (or Irish Constitution), arts 6, 15–27, 28–29, and 34–37. In the US context, see US Constitution, arts 1, 2, and 3. In the UK context, see the statement of Lord Templeman that 'Parliament makes the law, the executive carry the law into effect and the judiciary enforce the law' *In Re M* [1993] 3 WLR 433.

8 *The Federalist* No 47 (James Madison).

9 Walter Mondale, Robert Stein, and Caitlinrose Fisher, 'No Longer a Neutral Magistrate: The Foreign Intelligence Surveillance Court in the Wake of the War on Terror' (2016) 100 *Minnesota Law Review* 2251, 2255, citing Frederick Schwarz and Aziz Huq, *Unchecked and Unbalanced* (New Press 2007) 2. Due to their possession of 'Force, Will, and "Judgment"', the US executive branch has been described as 'the most dangerous branch'. Michael Stokes Paulsen, 'The Most Dangerous Branch: Executive Power to Say What the Law Is' (1994) 83(2) *The Georgetown Law Journal* 217, 219–220.

10 Anthony King, *The British Constitution* (Oxford University Press 2007) 12.

11 Irish Constitution, art 28; Anthony King, *The British Constitution* (Oxford University Press 2007) 6.

12 King argues that '[w]hat Britain lacks is not a written constitution but a codified Constitution, a Constitution with a capital "C", one that has been formally adopted'. Anthony King, *The British Constitution* (Oxford University Press 2007) 5.

of judicial review.[13] While it is necessary to note that parliamentary sovereignty remains a key concept in UK constitutional theory,[14] it should be noted that constitutional reforms in the UK have greatly increased the power of the judiciary in recent decades.[15] Of particular note has been the establishment of the Supreme Court[16] and the passage of the Human Rights Act 1998 which empowers judges to 'read' legislation 'in a way which is compatible with the European Convention of Human Rights and to declare laws to be "incompatible" with ECHR rights'.[17] Moreover, the UK is required to give effect to directly applicable European Union law (for as long as it remains a member).[18] Accordingly, in each jurisdiction, the judicial branch will often act as a vital check on executive power.[19]

13 In *Marbury v Madison* the US Supreme Court held that 'an Act of the Legislature repugnant to the Constitution is void' *Marbury v Madison* 5 US (1 Cranch) 137 (1803). Under Article 34.3.2° of the Irish Constitution, the superior courts are empowered to determine the 'validity of any law having regard to the provisions of this Constitution'. See also the special provision for pre-enactment constitutional review under Article 26 of the Irish Constitution.

14 Peter Leyland, *The Constitution of the United Kingdom: A Contextual Analysis* (2nd edn, Bloomsbury 2012) 26–32; Helen Fenwick, Gavin Phillipson, and Alexander Williams, *Text, Cases and Materials on Public Law and Human Rights* (4th edn, Routledge 2017) 13.

15 Robert Hazell, 'The Continuing Dynamism of Constitutional Reform' (2007) 60(1) *Parliamentary Affairs* 3, 17.

16 Constitutional Reform Act 2005.

17 Human Rights Act 1998, ss 3–4. A declaration of incompatibility 'does not affect the validity, continuing operation or enforcement' of the legislation. Vernon Bogdanor, 'Our New Constitution' (2004) 120 *Law Quarterly Review* 242.

18 As stated by the Court of Justice of the European Union in *Costa v Enel*, 'the Member States have limited their sovereign rights, albeit it within limited fields, and have thus created a body of law that binds both their nationals and themselves'. *Costa v Enel* [1964] ECR 585, 593–594. Ireland is also a Party to the ECHR and a Member State of the EU. Under the European Convention on Human Rights Act 2003, Irish courts must interpret the law in a manner compatible with the State's obligations under the ECHR in so far as is possible and must take judicial notice of judgments of the European Court of Human Rights. The superior courts may also make a declaration of incompatibility in a manner similar to the UK courts. This is quite different from a declaration of unconstitutionality which if made by the Irish superior courts renders the relevant law invalid. Article 29.4.6° of the Irish Constitution states that

> No provision of this Constitution invalidates laws enacted, acts done or measures adopted by the State . . . that are necessitated by the obligations of membership of the European Union referred to in subsection 5° of this section, or prevents laws enacted, acts done or measures adopted by . . . the said European Union.

19 David Gwynn Morgan, 'The Separation of Powers in Ireland' (1988) 7 *Saint Louis University Public Law Review* 257, 274.

The first chapter of this book examines the case study of encryption as it brings together many of the core themes of the book and provides a useful illustration of a technology that can place technical limits on the exercise of government power. Notably, Chapter 1 considers how technology comprehension gaps can be exploited and how metaphor and sensationalist rhetoric can be employed by those who favour the passage of anti-privacy encryption-restricting legislation. The second chapter of this book considers the case of the US Fourth Amendment and the associated third-party doctrine. This chapter and its discussion of the recent Supreme Court ruling in *Carpenter v United States* provides insight into the role of judicial interpretation in determining the boundaries of rights in the digital age. Chapter 3 begins by considering how secret definitions of important terms that are internal to the executive branch can mislead the public and allow intelligence activities to be carried out free from scrutiny. The chapter moves on to consider how the legality test as applied by the European Court of Human Rights has implications for this practice. Chapter 4 considers the more limited role the judicial branch tends to play in the surveillance context and considers the implications of secrecy for the effectiveness of judicial power. Chapter 5 draws together several strings of the argument regarding the relationship between the legislative and executive branch in the surveillance sphere. In particular, the chapter considers the tendency of the legislature to abdicate responsibility to the executive branch – and its agents – in the area of surveillance. The chapter first considers the UK's Investigatory Powers Act and the folly of blind adhesion to the principle of 'future proofed' legislation.[20] Second, the chapter discusses the stealth expansion of the Irish Public Services Card without an adequate legal basis and the obfuscation of government representatives – and law-makers – in their communications regarding the scheme.

The power to interpret the law – to 'say what the law is'[21] – is determinative of the 'construction and scope of all other governmental powers and of individual rights'.[22] Interpretation involves choices. Sometimes it involves a succession of choices. In legal interpretation, these choices will often be founded on doctrinal methods and allegiance to democratic and constitutional principles. At other times, ambiguity in meaning, at the definitional level can lead to choices being made on the basis of personal experiences,

20 Graham Smith, 'Future-proofing the Investigatory Powers Bill' (*Cyberleagle*, 15 April 2016) <www.cyberleagle.com/2016/04/future-proofing-investigatory-powers.html>
21 *Marbury v Madison* 5 US (1 Cranch) 137, 177 (1803).
22 Michael Stokes Paulsen, 'The Most Dangerous Branch: Executive Power to Say What the Law Is' (1994) 83(2) *The Georgetown Law Journal* 217, 220.

perspectives, and political agendas. As the party who interprets the law effectively determines what the law is, the interpretive power is a significant one. While the judicial branch may be primarily associated with the interpretive power, the concept of interpretation is a fluid one, and at times it is clear that the act of interpretation can resemble an act of law-making. Another example of functional fluidity between the branches of government is found where provision is made for limited rule-making capabilities by executive authorities. Moreover, through their exercise of executive functions, those implementing the law – or executing it – must also, in a sense, interpret the law in order to apply it at a practical level.[23] Depending on how the power of concrete application is used (or abused) by the executive branch, its members may, in effect, be engaging in a form of interpretation; and, in turn, in a limited form of law-making. While the laws of the legislature and the opinions of the judiciary are designed to guide the executive as they carry out their functions, greyness in the law is resolved by those operating on the ground.

The aim of this book is not to delve into the nuances and distinctions between the jurisdictions of the chosen case studies, but rather to examine the surveillance practices from the perspective of the principled commonalities shared by the US, UK, and Irish institutions. The Constitutions of both Ireland and the US provide for the protection of privacy,[24] and the UK and Ireland are parties to the European Convention on Human Rights which protects the 'right to respect for private life'. As both Ireland and the UK are currently Member States of the EU, the rights to the protection of private life[25] and protection of personal data[26] as set out in the Charter of Fundamental Rights provide additional support. Each jurisdiction also holds the rule of law to be a foundational value. Although the rule of law is a contested concept,[27] interpreted differently in different legal traditions, the

---

23 In the US context, Paulsen describes this as 'the ancillary power of Judgment'. Michael Stokes Paulsen, 'The Most Dangerous Branch: Executive Power to Say What the Law Is' (1994) 83(2) *The Georgetown Law Journal* 217, 220.

24 Irish courts have recognised an unenumerated right to privacy in the Irish Constitution. See, for example, *Kennedy v Ireland* [1987] IR 587 (HC). Different privacy rights are deemed to be protected by the First, Third, and Fifth Amendments of the US Constitution, but the Fourth Amendment prohibition against unreasonable search and seizure is the most relevant protection in the surveillance context. See Chapter 2 for more discussion.

25 CFR, art 7.

26 CFR, art 8.

27 Tamanaha suggests that the rule of law stands 'in the peculiar state of being the preeminent legitimating political ideal in the world today, without agreement upon precisely what it means'. Brian Tamanaha, *On the Rule of Law: History, Politics, Theory* (Cambridge

United Nations has provided some guidance that is useful when considering the importance of the principle across different jurisdictions:

> The 'rule of law' . . . refers to a principle of governance in which all persons, institutions and entities, public and private, including the State itself, are accountable to laws that are publicly promulgated, equally enforced and independently adjudicated, and which are consistent with international human rights norms and standards. It requires, as well, measures to ensure adherence to the principles of supremacy of law, equality before the law, accountability to the law, fairness in the application of the law, separation of powers, participation in decision-making, legal certainty, avoidance of arbitrariness, and procedural and legal transparency.[28]

In pursuit of constraining government power, the rule of law requires that laws are publically promulgated, independently adjudicated, provide transparency, and legal certainty. In spite of these shared values, the Snowden revelations demonstrated that the institutions and norms that were established to uphold the rule of law, democratic procedures, and 'relations between state and civil society' have not been functioning effectively in the surveillance context.[29] While privacy, human rights, and the rule of law 'have become deeply entrenched, even if imperfectly achieved, principles of modern societies', these achievements have been undermined by actions undertaken in secret.[30] This book proceeds on the premise that '[c]ivil liberties and protecting homeland security are bound together, not inevitable foes', and that '[o]pen government and loyalty are allies rather than tools of subversion'.[31]

University Press 2004) 4. In addition to its precise meaning being debated, the rule of law has also been critiqued as a tool of the current holders of power, see Tamanaha, 73–90.

28 United Nations, Report of the Secretary-General on the rule of law and transitional justice in conflict and post-conflict societies, UN Doc. S/2004/616, 4 <www.un.org/ruleoflaw/files/2004%20 report.pdf>. See also Karen Gebbia-Pinetti, 'Statutory Interpretation, Democratic Legitimacy and Legal-System Values' (1997) 21 *Seton Hall Legislative Journal* 233, 236–237.

29 Zygmunt Bauman, Didier Bigo, Paulo Esteves, Elspeth Guild, Vivienne Jabri, David Lyon, and Rob Walker, 'After Snowden: Rethinking the Impact of Surveillance' (2014) 8 *International Political Sociology* 121, 122.

30 Zygmunt Bauman, Didier Bigo, Paulo Esteves, Elspeth Guild, Vivienne Jabri, David Lyon, and Rob Walker, 'After Snowden: Rethinking the Impact of Surveillance' (2014) 8 *International Political Sociology* 121, 134.

31 Walter Mondale, Robert Stein, and Caitlinrose Fisher, 'No Longer a Neutral Magistrate: The Foreign Intelligence Surveillance Court in the Wake of the War on Terror' (2016) 100 *Minnesota Law Review* 2251, 2253.

1 Lost in translation and exploitation

The case of encryption

Encryption and power

It is clear that 'secrecy is a form of power'.[1] While an individual may not always need to keep secrets in order to be autonomous, the possession of the ability to keep secrets is vital if individuals are to make truly autonomous choices.[2] As a central theme of this book concerns the relationship between surveillance and power, the debate over encryption provides the ideal case study to begin the analysis. The use of encryption has, after all, been at the centre of the clash between the individual's power to keep secrets from the state and the state's power to penetrate those secrets for several decades.[3] Encryption has been defined as a 'process of converting messages, information, or data into a form unreadable by anyone except the intended recipient'.[4] The purpose of this process is to protect the 'confidentiality and integrity' of the encrypted information whether 'in transit' or 'at rest'.[5] Where 'end-to-end' encryption is applied, only the

1 Sisslea Bok, *Secrets: On the Ethics of Concealment and Revelation* (Pantheon Books 1982) 6; Michael Froomkin, 'Metaphor is the Key: Cryptography, the Clipper Chip, and the Constitution' (1995) 143 *University of Pennsylvania Law Review* 709, 712.
2 Kim Lane Scheppele, *Legal Secrets: Equality and Efficiency in the Common Law* (The University of Chicago Press, 1988) 302; Michael Froomkin, 'Metaphor is the Key: Cryptography, the Clipper Chip, and the Constitution' (1995) 143 *University of Pennsylvania Law Review* 709, 712.
3 Michael Froomkin, 'Metaphor Is the Key: Cryptography, the Clipper Chip, and the Constitution' (1995) 143 *University of Pennsylvania Law Review* 709, 712.
4 SANS Institute, *History of Encryption* (Cmd 730, 2001) <www.sans.org/reading-room/whitepapers/vpns/history-encryption-730>; Maria Helen Murphy, 'Technological Solutions to Privacy Questions: What Is the Role of Law?' (2016) 25(1) *Information & Communications Technology Law* 4, 11–12.
5 UNHRC, Twenty Ninth Session 25 May 2015 'Report of the Special Rapporteur on the Promotion and Protection of the Right to Freedom of Opinion and Expression,

sender and the recipient of the message can read the communication.[6] By designing a system to provide end-to-end encryption, technology companies are unable to comply with lawfully obtained warrants. Due to the issues this situation creates for investigative authorities, some call for the implementation of 'backdoors' into encrypted systems. A backdoor is a 'secondary way of accessing the encrypted content without breaking the encryption'.[7] Unfortunately, however, introducing backdoors to a system 'amounts to creating a system with a built-in flaw' that can be exploited by unauthorised third parties.[8]

To appreciate the significance of the ongoing encryption debate, it is important to briefly consider the historical context behind the ancient science of secret communication – cryptography – of which encryption is a vital branch.[9] It has been remarked that '[c]ryptography rearranges power' and attempts at cryptography – or coded messaging – are believed to be almost as old as communication itself.[10] Throughout its history, cryptography has often been used to shield communications from powerful third parties. In the military context, efforts to develop unbreakable codes for the communication of sensitive information and to interpret the codes of enemy actors have been as intense as any conventional arms-race. The strategic importance of securing your secrets and exposing the secrets of others has been evident from the use of transposition ciphers by Lacedaemonian generals, to the war efforts of the cryptanalysts at Bletchley Park,

David Kaye'. UN Doc A/HRC/29/32; Maria Helen Murphy, 'Technological Solutions to Privacy Questions: What Is the Role of Law?' (2016) 25(1) *Information & Communications Technology Law* 4, 11–12. Other reasons for encrypting data include authentication, and nonrepudiation. Alfred Menezes, Jonathan Katz, Paul van Oorschot, and Scott Vanstone, *Handbook of Applied Cryptography* (CRC Press 1997) 4; Jeffrey Vagle, 'Furtive Encryption: Power, Trust, and the Constitutional Cost of Collective Surveillance' (2015) 90(1) *Indiana Law Journal* 101, 103–104, 117.

  6 Hugh McCarthy, 'Decoding the Encryption Debate: Why Legislating to Restrict Strong Encryption will not Resolve the "Going Dark" Problem' (2016) 20(3) *Journal of Internet Law* 1, 18.

  7 Hugh McCarthy, 'Decoding the Encryption Debate: Why Legislating to Restrict Strong Encryption will not Resolve the "Going Dark" Problem' (2016) 20(3) *Journal of Internet Law* 1, 19.

  8 Jeffrey Vagle and Matt Blaze, 'Security "Front Doors" vs "Backdoors": A Distinction Without a Difference' (*Just Security*, 17 October 2014) <www.justsecurity.org/16503/security-front-doors-vs-back-doors-distinction-difference/>

  9 Laurence Smith, *Cryptography: Science of Secret Writing* (Dover 1955).

 10 Phillip Rogaway, 'The Moral Character of Cryptographic Work' (Essay delivered for the IACR Distinguished Lecture at Asiacrypt, Auckland, 2 December 2015) <web.cs.ucdavis.edu/~rogaway/papers/moral-fn.pdf>

to the activities of the world's intelligence agencies today.[11] In this context, knowledge is, indeed, power.

Shifts in power and the 'Crypto Wars'

Even though modern encryption techniques initially developed in the hands of competing governments seeking military or political advantage, it is now clear that encryption is an important tool for all of society.[12] The central role of the internet in modern trade, communication, and commercial transactions has necessitated the growth of encryption and its widespread adoption. While encryption offers many benefits and has been crucial to the success and expansion of the internet, any technology that enables an individual to shield the contents of their communications or stored data from malicious actors can also be used to hinder lawful government access to information. There is a clear tension between an individual's interest in maintaining the secrecy of certain information through the use of encryption and the State's interest in having no spaces immune from lawful authority. Vagle characterises the right to privacy in this context as having 'everything to do with delineating the legitimate limits of governmental power'.[13]

As encryption moved from a tool solely for the most powerful, governments and law enforcement agencies attempted to resist the democratisation of the technology – notably during the 1990s 'Crypto War'. One of the first approaches adopted by the US Government to restrict the availability of encryption was to introduce export restrictions by placing certain types of encryption on the Munitions List.[14] Importantly, the export restrictions also had implications for the domestic development and use of encryption. The global market for technological products meant that many US-based companies opted to use the same (lower) standard of encryption in the domestic market as was used for the export market in order to take account of

---

11 Laurence Smith, *Cryptography: Science of Secret Writing* (Dover 1955) 16–20; Francis Harry Hinsley and Alan Stripp (eds), *Codebreakers: The Inside Story of Bletchley Park* (Oxford University Press 1993); Susan Landau, *Listening In: Cybersecurity in an Insecure Age* (Yale University Press 2017).

12 Maria Helen Murphy, 'Technological Solutions to Privacy Questions: What Is the Role of Law?' (2016) 25(1) *Information & Communications Technology Law* 4, 12; Gordon Corera, *Intercept: The Secret History of Computers and Spies* (Weidenfeld & Nicholson 2015) 104–105.

13 Jeffrey Vagle, 'Furtive Encryption: Power, Trust, and the Constitutional Cost of Collective Surveillance' (2015) 90(1) *Indiana Law Journal* 101, 108.

14 Sharon Black, *Telecommunications Law in the Internet Age* (Morgan Kauffman 2002) 353.

production costs and design considerations.[15] Unsurprisingly, the suboptimal market conditions led to serious industry opposition and the export
controls were relaxed over time.[16]

In another attempt to place controls on encryption, the US Government
devised the 'Clipper Chip' programme in the 1990s. This initiative encour-
aged companies to voluntarily install NSA-designed microchips into the
communications hardware that they manufactured.[17] The intention behind the
programme was that government agencies would be able to gain access to
encrypted communications through a system described as 'key-escrow'. The
plan was to allow government agencies to access decrypted communications
by demonstrating appropriate legal authority to secure entities that would hold
the keys capable of unlocking the encrypted communications.[18] The proposal
was met with immediate resistance and the Clipper Chip programme failed
to gain significant support or uptake by either consumers or manufacturers.[19]

While overt opposition to encryption was side-lined for a time, the debate
has returned to the mainstream in recent years. From the summer of 2013,
the Snowden revelations have been hailed as a turning point in the global
debate on privacy and surveillance.[20] The released documents provided

15 Susan Landau, 'Under the Radar: NSA's Efforts to Secure Private-Sector Telecommunications Infrastructure' (2014) 7 *Journal of National Security Law & Policy* 411, 411, 423;
Maria Helen Murphy, 'Technological Solutions to Privacy Questions: What Is the Role of
Law?' (2016) 25(1) *Information & Communications Technology Law* 4, 13.
16 Susan Landau, 'Under the Radar: NSA's Efforts to Secure Private-Sector Telecommunications Infrastructure' (2014) 7 *Journal of National Security Law & Policy* 411, 425; Revi-
sions to Encryption Items, 15 CFR ss 734, 740, 742, 770, 772, and 774. Notably, in a case
involving a US academic who had been prevented from publishing an encryption program
on the Internet, the Ninth Circuit Court of Appeals found that code was protected speech
under the First Amendment of the US Constitution. *Bernstein et al v United States Department of State et al* (1996) 922 F Supp 1426. Maria Helen Murphy, 'Technological Solutions
to Privacy Questions: What Is the Role of Law?' (2016) 25(1) *Information & Communications Technology Law* 4, 13.
17 Presidential Directive Authorizing the Clipper Initiative (Declassified Document Obtained
by the Electronic Privacy Information Center under the Freedom of Information Act 1993);
Maria Helen Murphy, 'Technological Solutions to Privacy Questions: What Is the Role of
Law?' (2016) 25(1) *Information & Communications Technology Law* 4, 14.
18 Presidential Directive Authorizing the Clipper Initiative (Declassified Document Obtained
by the Electronic Privacy Information Center under the Freedom of Information Act 1993).
19 Harold Abelson, Ross Anderson, Steven Bellovin, Josh Benaloh, Matt Blaze, Whitfield
Diffie, John Gilmore, Peter Neumann, Ronald Rivest, Jeffrey Schiller, and Bruce Schneier,
'The Risks of Key Recovery, Key Escrow, and Trusted Third-Party Encryption' (Columbia
University Academic Commons 1997) <https://doi.org/10.7916/D8GM8F2W>
20 Glenn Greenwald, *No Place to Hide: Edward Snowden, the NSA, and the US Surveillance State* (Metropolitan Books 2014); Maria Helen Murphy, 'The Pendulum Effect:

remarkable insight into the covert activities of global intelligence agencies. While experts had discussed the likely existence of such capabilities, the documented proof provided by the Snowden leaks provided a level of tangibility, detail, and non-deniability that was difficult for the general public to ignore.[21] One illustration of heightened privacy awareness in the post-Snowden world is the increased level of marketing and uptake of privacy enhancing technologies at the consumer level.[22] The central role of consumer focused encryption solutions in this movement is at least partially attributable to Edward Snowden. A key theme of Snowden's earlier public statements was that 'encryption works'.[23]

In spite of a reported shift in public attitudes following the Snowden revelations, legislative reforms have been minor, and in some cases, even deleterious to privacy. Notwithstanding this, increased consumer interest in privacy has disturbed many in intelligence circles. James Comey, the former Director of the Federal Bureau of Investigation, has even suggested that the pendulum on privacy issues has 'swung too far' against surveillance interests.[24] Not only did the Snowden disclosures expose the vast intelligence capabilities and appetite of government agencies, but they also displayed the vast 'surveillant assemblage' comprised of government and commercial information collection. Following an initial scramble in the face of criticism on this point, many technology companies condemned government surveillance and positioned themselves as anti-surveillance allies of privacy advocates.[25]

Comparisons Between the Snowden Revelations and the Church Committee. What are the Potential Implications for Europe?' (2014) 23(2) *Information & Communications Technology Law* 192.

21 Maria Helen Murphy, 'The Pendulum Effect: Comparisons Between the Snowden Revelations and the Church Committee. What are the Potential Implications for Europe?' (2014) 23(2) *Information & Communications Technology Law* 192.

22 While such products are often not as secure as their endorsers assert, the increased visibility of these products suggests an appetite for technological solutions to privacy questions. Maria Helen Murphy, 'The Pendulum Effect: Comparisons between the Snowden Revelations and the Church Committee. What are the Potential Implications for Europe?' (2014) 23(2) *Information & Communications Technology Law* 192; Maria Helen Murphy, 'Technological Solutions to Privacy Questions: What Is the Role of Law?' (2016) 25(1) *Information & Communications Technology Law* 4, 4–5.

23 Glenn Greenwald, 'Edward Snowden: NSA Whistleblower Answers Reader Questions' *The Guardian* (London, 17 June 2013) <www.theguardian.com/world/2013/jun/17/edward-snowden-nsa-files-whistleblower?CMP=twt_gu>

24 James Comey, 'Going Dark: Are Technology, Privacy, and Public Safety on a Collision Course?' (FBI, 16 October 2014) <www.fbi.gov/news/speeches/going-dark-are-technology-privacy-and-public-safety-on-a-collision-course>

25 Maria Helen Murphy, 'Technological Solutions to Privacy Questions: What Is the Role of Law?' (2016) 25(1) *Information & Communications Technology Law* 4, 15.

While the first Crypto War affirmed the importance of encryption for internet security and illustrated how cryptography had moved on from its military past, the more recent growth in consumer-friendly encryption products and services is an important signal of citizen intent to take back control over their data. A common criticism of encryption is that it can be difficult for the non-technologically savvy user to utilise, but many companies seem eager to address this gap in the market. Apple is one of the most prominent endorsers of user friendly encryption and the company sparked renewed interest in the consumer use of encryption in September 2014 when their CEO, Tim Cook, touted Apple's ability to stymie government data requests.[26]

Apple would do this by designing its newer products in a manner that denies Apple access to encrypted customer information held on devices.[27] Apple's pro-encryption policies have been subject to much criticism by government actors.[28] In spite of the increased uptake of consumer encryption, for some a perception remains that encryption – outside of its commercial or government applications – is inherently suspicious. A notable example of this was exposed in documents released by Edward Snowden that revealed the NSA's position that permitted the collection and indefinite storage of any information obtained from 'domestic communications for cryptanalytic purposes'.[29] As pointed out by Vagle, this effectively meant that 'the mere fact that data is encrypted' was 'alone enough to give the NSA the right to store that data (regardless of its US or foreign origin) and hold it for as long as it takes to decrypt it'.[30]

---

26 Craig Timberg, 'Apple will no Longer Unlock most iPhones, iPads for Police, even with Search Warrants' *The Washington Post* (Washington, 18 September 2014) <www.washing tonpost.com/business/technology/2014/09/17/2612af58-3ed2-11e4-b03f-de718edeb92f_ story.html>. Other companies that announced renewed commitment to implement end-to-end encryption on a default basis include Google, Facebook, WhatsApp, and BlackBerry. Hugh McCarthy, 'Decoding the Encryption Debate: Why Legislating to Restrict Strong Encryption will not Resolve the "Going Dark" Problem' (2016) 20(3) *Journal of Internet Law* 1, 21.

27 Rónán Kennedy and Maria Helen Murphy, *Information and Communications Technology Law in Ireland* (Clarus 2017) 225. Craig Timberg, 'Apple will no Longer Unlock most iPhones, iPads for Police, even with Search Warrants' *The Washington Post* (Washington, 18 September 2014).

28 Something of a 'red-queen's race' has developed between Apple and law enforcement agencies. See, for example, recent efforts by Apple to counteract strategies adopted by the authorities, Jack Nicas, 'Apple to Close iPhone Security Hole that Law Enforcement Uses to Crack Devices' *The New York Times* (New York, 15 June 2018) <www.nytimes. com/2018/06/13/technology/apple-iphone-police.html>

29 See NSA, Exhibit B: Minimization Procedures used by the National Security Agency in Connection with Accusations of Foreign Intelligence Information (2007) <www.theguard ian.com/world/interactive/2013/jun/20/exhibit-b-nsa-procedures-document>

30 Jeffrey Vagle, 'Furtive Encryption: Power, Trust, and the Constitutional Cost of Collective Surveillance' (2015) 90(1) *Indiana Law Journal* 101, 103–104.

Language and encryption

Differences of opinion regarding the 'correct' interpretation of language frequently arise in law. While much of what makes the relationship between language and power in the surveillance context worthy of inquiry rests on the secrecy that surrounds surveillance measures, an additional factor that cannot be underestimated is the technical nature of the subject matter. It is problematic where language is manipulated or interpreted in a way that circumvents or limits rights. The problem of restricting rights is exacerbated where the rights are limited in a manner that is obscured as citizens are denied the opportunity to protest or demand recalibration. The opportunity for manipulation increases in the context of technology where genuine understanding tends to rest with a cloistered few.

It is widely recognised that a significant proportion of the general population does not fully understand the implications of much technology that is crucial to everyday life. At times, those with the relevant knowledge seek to exploit this advantage by encouraging disengagement with the broader effects such technologies may have on other issues about which the public has an interest. Moreover, lawyers – as a general class – are often accused of technological naivety and of blithely creating (in the case of drafters and policy advisors) and applying (in the case of the judiciary) laws that fundamentally misunderstand technology.[31] In the area of encryption policy, there has been a perceived lack of know-how associated with law-makers worldwide. Amber Rudd – speaking as the UK Home Secretary at the time – provides just one example of this with her statement that 'real people' do not need encryption.[32] The metaphor is a popular tool of legal thinkers as a means of explanation, persuasion, and analysis. While this type of reasoning is clearly evidenced in all areas of the law – not least by the analogical reasoning central to the common law system – metaphors can be particularly helpful when grappling with complex technological concepts.

---

31 Tim Cushing, 'An ongoing Lack of Technical Prowess is Resulting in Bad Laws, Bad Prosecutions, and Bad Judicial Decisions' (*Techdirt*, 28 September 2016) <www.techdirt.com/articles/20160926/10113735633/ongoing-lack-technical-prowess-is-resulting-bad-laws-bad-prosecutions-bad-judicial-decisions.shtml>; Danny Yadron, 'US Efforts to Regulate Encryption have been Flawed, Government Report Finds' *The Guardian* (London, 30 June 2016) <www.theguardian.com/technology/2016/jun/29/government-encryption-regulation-report-criticism>; Dylan Byers, 'Senate Fails its Zuckerberg Test' (*CNN Tech*, 11 April 2018) <money.cnn.com/2018/04/10/technology/senate-mark-zuckerberg-testimony/index.html>

32 Amber Rudd, 'We don't want to Ban Encryption, but our Inability to see what Terrorists Are Plotting Undermines our Security' *The Telegraph* (London, 31 July 2017) <www.telegraph.co.uk/news/2017/07/31/dont-want-ban-encryption-inability-see-terrorists-plotting-online/>

As the choice of metaphor favoured by an interpreter or communicator can be decisive – and as those in power typically 'get to impose their metaphors'[33] – there is a need for caution. While the use of metaphor can be a helpful tool to illuminate abstract or technical concepts, the ability of metaphors to 'colour' and control our subsequent thinking about a subject is particularly powerful when used to describe new technologies.[34] Froomkin demonstrates the significance of the choice by showing how using a metaphor of communication (eg 'encryption as language'[35]) to characterise encryption as opposed to a metaphor of exclusion (eg 'encryption as a safe'[36]) can have significant legal effects.[37] While these metaphors serve as interpretive tools designed to reason out the legal implications of encryption and encryption restriction, it is notable that technical terms associated with encryption are also littered with metaphors, from the encryption 'key' to the 'backdoor'. While metaphors can elucidate concepts for those unfamiliar, there is a risk that over time these tools can become 'intellectual crutches' that oversimply the critical issues.[38]

The technology knowledge gap is vulnerable to exploitation by those who wish to retain and enhance the powers of investigative agencies at all costs and specifically at the expense of the privacy of the general public. When speaking to non-expert audiences, it is logical for experts with strategic goals and interests to choose metaphors inclined to persuade the non-expert party to support their position. While this is not necessarily a problem in itself, it becomes an issue where the choice of metaphor distorts the reality. As argued by Gill, by 'obfuscating certain characteristics and emphasizing

33 George Lakoff and Mark Johnson, *Metaphors We Live By* (The University of Chicago Press 1980) 157.
34 Michael Froomkin, 'Metaphor Is the Key: Cryptography, the Clipper Chip, and the Constitution' (1995) 143 *University of Pennsylvania Law Review* 709, 859; Steven Winter, 'The Metaphor of Standing and the Problem of Self-Governance' (1988) 40(6) *Stanford Law Review* 1382, 1383.
35 Or 'encryption as a car'.
36 Or 'encryption as a house'.
37 Michael Froomkin, 'Metaphor Is the Key: Cryptography, the Clipper Chip, and the Constitution' (1995) 143 *University of Pennsylvania Law Review* 709, 862.
38 Jeffrey Vagle, 'Furtive Encryption: Power, Trust, and the Constitutional Cost of Collective Surveillance' (2015) 90(1) *Indiana Law Journal* 101, 117. Kiok has criticised 'the language that encryption companies often use to describe what their products "do" (e.g., creating encrypted "containers", encrypting a "file" or "folder", or using a "key" to "unlock" encrypted media)' for causing 'people to improperly analogize how encryption software actually works'. Jeffrey Kiok, 'Missing the Metaphor: Compulsory Decryption and the Fifth Amendment' (2015) 24(1) *Boston University Public Interest Law Journal* 53, 58.

others, the strategic deployment of a conceptual metaphor may subtly move the goalposts of a given argument, or it may change the game entirely'.[39]

It is particularly problematic where the distorting metaphor is delivered by a trusted party. The encryption debate has been notable for the simplification of technological issues. Supporters of restricted encryption employ misleading language in order to represent their positions as simple common sense. For example, when arguing for the creation of encryption backdoors in order to enable government access to encrypted communications, a politician may liken the issue to the intercepting of telephone calls with lawful authority. When making this comparison, the metaphor facilitates the transposition of an 'existing conceptual framework' without adequate consideration of key factual distinctions.[40]

It is interesting to note how the potency of the backdoor metaphor has worked against those who support limiting encryption as the use of encryption backdoors has been effectively likened to 'leaving keys under door mats; it is only a matter of time before they are discovered'.[41] As the potential security harms of backdoors have become clearer to the general public, the term has become loaded with negative connotations and those in favour of limiting encryption tend to avoid using the term. For example, in 2016 the US Attorney General at the time, Loretta Lynch, told the World Economic Forum that the US did not wish to insert security backdoors into encrypted communications, but merely to compel technology vendors and service providers to decrypt communications when required to do so by court order. As stated by Lynch:

> We in the US government are not asking for a backdoor. We're asking to work with Silicon Valley to make sure that as we preserve encryption we also preserve what we currently have, which is the ability for companies to respond to law enforcement warrants: court-ordered, court-authorized requests for information.[42]

39 Lex Gill, 'Law, Metaphor and the Encrypted Machine' (2018) 55(2) *Osgoode Hall Law Journal*; Jonas Ebbesson, 'Law, Power and Language: Beware of Metaphors' (2008) 53 *Scandinavian Studies in Law* 260.
40 Tim Hwang and Karen Levy, 'The Cloud and Other Dangerous Metaphors' *The Atlantic* (Boston, 20 January 2015).
41 Hugh McCarthy, 'Decoding the Encryption Debate: Why Legislating to Restrict Strong Encryption will not Resolve the "Going Dark" Problem' (2016) 20(3) *Journal of Internet Law* 1, 23.
42 Tim Greene, 'Despite Rhetoric, Department of Justice, NSA Still Seek Backdoors' (*Networkworld*, 25 January 2016) <www.networkworld.com/article/3026121/lan-wan/despite-rhetoric-doj-nsa-still-seek-backdoors.html>

This statement is misleading as there is yet to be discovered a method by which vendors and providers can decrypt customer data without introducing a backdoor 'of some sort'.[43] This communication tactic illustrates how a lack of technological understanding among the intended audience can be used to misrepresent the intrusive powers requested. A similar example is found in Lynch's separate assertion that she is in favour of 'strong encryption', but not 'warrant-proof encryption'.[44] This characterisation attempts to avoid engagement with the thorny questions of encryption by ignoring the technical realities, or in fact, by implying that the technical realities do not exist. In a search for legitimacy, Lynch misappropriates the term 'strong encryption', which is generally considered to mean 'unbreakable encryption'.[45] Or as Landau puts it, '[t]hat means encryption systems without backdoors, front doors, or any other form of easy access'.[46]

As the term 'backdoor' has become contentious, those in favour of undermining encryption seek to change the narrative by simply changing the language. Notably, the recently retired former Director of the NSA, Michael Rogers, rejects the term 'backdoor' and prefers to use the term 'front door' to describe encryption limiting measures where lawful authority is used.[47] Other terms used by encryption-restricting advocates instead of the term 'backdoor' include 'golden key', 'exceptional access', 'side door', and 'responsible encryption'.

---

43 It should be noted that some reject the impossibility narrative touted by some in the security community; Steven Levy, 'Cracking the Crypto War' (*Wired*, 2 December 2015) <www.wired.com/story/crypto-war-clear-encryption/>. It remains the case, however, that no solution has yet been successfully proven and as a result, it is misleading and potentially harmful for politicians to suggest that there is a simple technical solution readily available or that technology can always be made to bend to the law without unwanted negative effects. Tim Greene, 'Despite Rhetoric, Department of Justice, NSA Still Seek Backdoors' (*Network World*, 25 January 2016) <www.networkworld.com/article/3026121/lan-wan/despite-rhetoric-doj-nsa-still-seek-backdoors.html>

44 Oversight of the US Department of Justice Full Committee Hearing Senate Judiciary Committee: Wednesday, 9 March 2016 <www.judiciary.senate.gov/meetings/oversight-of-the-us-department-of-justice>; Gus Hosein, 'Compromising Over Technology, Security, and Privacy' (2017) 11(1) *International Journal of Communication* 902.

45 Bruce Schneier, 'The Importance of Strong Encryption to Security' (*Schneier on Security*, 25 February 2016) <www.schneier.com/blog/archives/2016/02/the_importance_.html>

46 Susan Landau, *Listening In: Cybersecurity in an Insecure Age* (Yale University Press 2017) Preface.

47 Ellen Nakashima and Barton Gellman, 'As Encryption Technology Spreads, US Spies and Law Enforcement Worry about Access to Data for Investigations' *The Washington Post* (Washington, 11 April 2015) <news.nationalpost.com/news/us-encryption-law-enforcemen-739351>; Maria Helen Murphy, 'Technological Solutions to Privacy Questions: What Is the Role of Law?' (2016) 25(1) *Information & Communications Technology Law* 4, 17.

Using these terms would appear to lend an additional level of credibility to the practice of undermining encryption, but as widely attested by security experts, the creation of backdoors – even if called by another name – will inevitably create vulnerabilities for all users that can be exploited by criminals and others operating without proper legal authority.[48]

Perhaps unsurprisingly, similar tactics were used by defenders of the UK Investigatory Powers Act provisions on encryption. When asked about the encryption limiting implications of the IPA clause requiring communications providers to remove electronic protection of data in certain circumstances, the then Home Secretary – now Prime Minister – Theresa May denied the government was seeking backdoors for intelligence agencies. May asserted that:

> We are not saying to them that the Government want keys to their encryption – no, absolutely not. (. . .) The Government do not need to know what the encryption is or to know the key to the encryption. It is exactly as you say, Chairman. If there is a lawful warrant requesting certain information, it is about that information being readable.[49]

In spite of this apparent assurance, when asked about the implications of the requirement for end-to-end encryption, May stated that:

> What we say to companies today and will say to companies under this legislation is that, when a warrant is lawfully served on them, there is an expectation that they will be able to take reasonable steps to ensure that they can comply with that warrant – i.e. that they can provide the information that has been requested under that lawful warrant in a form that is legible for the authorities.

This 'expectation' would appear to put the practice of end-to-end encryption on potentially shaky ground. When assessing the implications for end-to-end encryption under the IPA, it is important to consider the relevant

---

48 Harold Abelson, Ross Anderson, Steven Bellovin, Josh Benaloh, Matt Blaze, Whitfield Diffie, John Gilmore, Matthew Green, Susan Landau, Peter Neumann, Ronald Rivest, Jeffrey Schiller, Bruce Schneier, Michael Specter, and Daniel Weitzner, 'Keys Under Doormats: Mandating Insecurity by Requiring Government Access to all Data and Communications' (2015) 1(1) *Journal of Cybersecurity* 69. Maria Helen Murphy, 'Technological Solutions to Privacy Questions: What Is the Role of Law?' (2016) 25(1) *Information & Communications Technology Law* 4, 18.

49 Joint Committee on the Draft Investigatory Powers Bill, oral evidence: Draft Investigatory Powers Bill HC 651 (13 January 2016) 651 <data.parliament.uk/writtenevidence/committeeevidence.svc/evidencedocument/draft-investigatory-powers-bill-committee/draft-investigatory-powers-bill/oral/26875.html>

warrant and authorisation provisions in light of the state's power to issue a 'technical capability notice' (TCN) under section 253 IPA.[50] Telecommunications operators[51] have a duty to 'take all steps' necessary to give effect to interception warrants but are not required to take any steps which are not 'reasonably practicable for the relevant operator to take'.[52] This pragmatic approach is undermined, however, by the provision that

> Where obligations have been imposed on a relevant operator ('P') under section 253 (technical capability notices), for the purposes of subsection (4) the steps which it is reasonably practicable for P to take include every step which it would have been reasonably practicable for P to take if P had complied with all of those obligations.[53]

A TCN can be used to impose obligations on telecommunications operators to implement specific technical facilities where a Secretary of State considers it necessary to secure the assistance required on the basis of relevant legal authorisation.[54] The IPA provides that the obligations a TCN can impose on a telecommunications operator will be set out in regulations,[55]

---

50 A more limited form of TCN existed under section 12 of the Regulation of Investigatory Powers Act. It should be noted that regulations under RIPA provided for TCNs that would require Public Telecommunication Services to 'ensure that the person on whose application the interception warrant was issued is able to remove any electronic protection applied by the service provider to the intercepted communication and the related communications data'. The Regulation of Investigatory Powers (Maintenance of Interception Capability) Order 2002, SI 2002/193. In addition to the wider scope of the IPA, increased application of end-to-end encryption by communications providers means the implications are much more significant today; Graham Smith, 'Backdoors, Black Boxes and #IPAct Technical Capability Regulations' (*Cyberleagle*, 8 May 2017) <www.cyberleagle.com/2017/05/back-doors-black-boxes-and-ipact.html>

51 'Telecommunications operator' is broadly defined to include a person who '(a) offers or provides a telecommunications service to persons in the United Kingdom, or (b) controls or provides a telecommunication system which is (wholly or partly) – (i) in the United Kingdom, or (ii) controlled from the United Kingdom.' IPA, s 261.

52 IPA, s 43.

53 IPA, s 43(6).

54 See section 253 for detail on the circumstances under which a TCN can be issued, including the involvement of a Judicial Commissioner.

55 See The Investigatory Powers (Technical Capability) Regulations 2018, SI 2018/353 which includes the following language:

> To provide and maintain the capability to – (a) disclose the content of communications or secondary data in an intelligible form where reasonably practicable; (b) remove electronic protection applied by or on behalf of the telecommunications operator to the communications or data where reasonably practicable, or (c) to permit the person to whom a warrant is addressed to remove such electronic protection.

but the Act explicitly states that those obligations may include 'obligations relating to the removal by a relevant operator of electronic protection applied by or on behalf of that operator to any communications or data'.[56] Therefore, after some careful analysis, it becomes clear that it is possible to proactively compel telecommunications operators to implement technical solutions designed to undermine encryption. Crucially, while operators may only be required to take steps that are 'reasonably practicable', where a TCN has been imposed, the meaning of 'reasonably practicable' is deemed to mean 'every step which it would have been reasonably practicable for P to take *if* P had complied with all of those obligations' set out in the TCN.[57] This significantly alters what 'reasonably practicable' might be interpreted to mean in the abstract. McCarthy has suggested that the ambiguity regarding the implications of the IPA for end-to-end encryption is 'not the byproduct of technical oversight, but deliberately included'.[58]

Fear and rhetoric: debating encryption in the political sphere

In the debate on encryption, challenges of understanding have led to some distortion in the public discourse. The technology comprehension gap can also be used to the advantage of the rhetorician. When the proposal is a new surveillance measure, the plea for its necessity is often heightened by reference to the potential catastrophic effects of not being able to obtain necessary intelligence to combat crime and terrorism. Prominent advocates of encryption restriction continually warn of all intelligence 'going dark'.[59] Public statements of this sort illustrate how emotive language can be used to drive the debate and popular conception of an issue. The phrase 'going dark' is evocative and may seem ominous to the average citizen who wants to feel safe and views the actions of law enforcement as largely good and proper. In spite of this language, however, it has been effectively argued that law enforcement and other investigative authorities have in fact never

---

56 IPA, s 253(4)(5).
57 Emphasis added.
58 Hugh McCarthy, 'Decoding the Encryption Debate: Why Legislating to Restrict Strong Encryption will not Resolve the "Going Dark" Problem' (2016) 20(3) *Journal of Internet Law* 1, 29.
59 James Comey, 'Going Dark: Are Technology, Privacy, and Public Safety on a Collision Course?' (FBI, 16 October 2014) <www.fbi.gov/news/speeches/going-dark-are-technology-privacy-and-public-safety-on-a-collision-course>

had more access to personal data in all of history.[60] In fact, some have characterised the current situation as unmanageable due to the floods of data requiring analysis.[61]

Bruce Schneier warns against the sensationalist hype of the 'Four Horsemen of the information apocalypse: terrorists, drug dealers, kidnappers, and child pornographers'.[62] These archetypes are often alluded to by governments seeking to restrict individual privacy rights. Former UK Prime Minister, David Cameron, for example, advocated for limiting encryption in 2015 by arguing that terrorists should never have 'a safe space in which to communicate'.[63] The targeting of feared minority groups in order to pursue broader policy goals is, of course, not a new phenomenon, but it is particularly pervasive in the privacy context due to the intangibility of both elements of the proposed balancing test. Not only can privacy seem to be a relatively intangible right that an individual may be happy to trade until they experience the consequences of losing that privacy, but the unknowable nature of the security threat competing with privacy looms like a menacing spectre. A judicial example of such thinking is found in the famously overturned[64] US Supreme Court decision of *Olmstead v United States*, where the 'organization, scale, enterprise, and success' of the criminal enterprise that was the focus of the case provided 'the occasion for a morality tale in which

60 Peter Swire, 'The Golden Age of Surveillance' *Slate* (New York, 15 July 2015) <www.slate.com/articles/technology/future_tense/2015/07/encryption_back_doors_aren_t_necessary_we_re_already_in_a_golden_age_of.html>

61 Peter Maass, 'Inside NSA, Officials Privately Criticize "Collect It All" Surveillance' *The Intercept* (New York, 28 May 2015); Melissa De Zwart, Sal Humphreys, and Beatrix Van Dissel, 'Surveillance, Big Data and Democracy: Lessons for Australia from the US and UK' (2014) 37(2) *University of New South Wales Law Journal* 713, 717.

62 Bruce Schneier, 'Computer Crime Hype' (*Schneier on Security*, 16 December 2005) <www.schneier.com/blog/archives/2005/12/computer_crime_1.html>

63 Adam Bienkov, 'David Cameron: Twitter and Facebook Privacy is Unsustainable' (*Politics*, 30 June 2015) <www.politics.co.uk/news/2015/06/30/david-cameron-twitter-and-facebookprivacy-is-unsustainable>. UK law provides for the mandatory disclosure of encryption keys in certain circumstances. Regulation of Investigatory Powers Act 2000, s 49. This language has also been used by Prime Minister Theresa May and former Home Secretary Amber Rudd. Alex Hern, 'May Calls Again for Tech Firms to Act on Encrypted Messaging' *The Guardian* (London, 25 January 2018) <www.theguardian.com/technology/2018/jan/25/theresa-may-calls-tech-firms-act-encrypted-messaging>; Alex Hern, 'UK Government can Force Encryption Removal, but Fears Losing, Experts Say' *The Guardian* (London, 29 March 2017) <www.theguardian.com/technology/2017/mar/29/uk-government-encryption-whatsapp-investigatory-powers-act>

64 *Katz v United States* 389 US 347 (1967).

the government represents good struggling against the forces of evil'.[65] Where actions are 'painted as enormous threats', privacy protections – whether found in a domestic constitution or in an international human rights document – can be made to seem irrelevant.[66] Froomkin cautioned in 1995 that

> [g]iven the public opposition to Clipper, the government is unlikely to propose mandatory key escrow without some triggering event. In the wake of a great crime, perhaps by terrorists or drug cartels – the detection of which could plausibly have been frustrated by encryption – that which today looks clearly unconstitutional might unfortunately appear more palatable.[67]

Froomkin's prediction was well-founded and as was illustrated by the response to the September 11 attacks, the fear of a terrorist attack on domestic soil is often the most powerful influence over public opinion.[68]

Government insiders seem all too aware of the potency of such events and how they can be utilised in order to gain popular support. In a 2015 email by an NSA lawyer, Robert Litt, this reasoning was made explicit. Litt expressed disappointment at the White House's decision not to pursue anti-encryption legislation and posited that the position 'could turn in the event of a terrorist attack or criminal event where strong encryption can be shown to have hindered law enforcement'.[69] Litt expressed the belief that there was value in

65 See discussion of *Olmstead v United States* 277 US 438 (1928) 277 in James White, 'Judicial Criticism' (1986) 20(4) *Georgia Law Review* 835, 854; Michael Froomkin, 'Metaphor Is the Key: Cryptography, the Clipper Chip, and the Constitution' (1995) 143 *University of Pennsylvania Law Review* 709, 859.
66 Michael Froomkin, 'Metaphor Is the Key: Cryptography, the Clipper Chip, and the Constitution' (1995) 143 *University of Pennsylvania Law Review* 709, 859.
67 Michael Froomkin, 'Metaphor Is the Key: Cryptography, the Clipper Chip, and the Constitution' (1995) 143 *University of Pennsylvania Law Review* 709, 850.
68 The manner in which the USA PATRIOT Act was rushed through Congress following the September 11 attacks is often cited as an example of intelligence interests capitalising on the 'security at all costs' sentiment that strengthens in times of crisis. Uniting and Strengthening America by Providing Appropriate Tools Required to Intercept and Obstruct Terrorism Act 2001 Public Law 107–156; Beryl Howell, 'Seven Weeks: The Making of the USA Patriot Act' (2003–2004) 72 *George Washington Law Review* 1145; Rónán Kennedy and Maria Helen Murphy, *Information and Communications Technology Law in Ireland* (Clarus 2017) 200; Christopher Slobogin, *Privacy at Risk: The New Government Surveillance and the Fourth Amendment* (The University of Chicago Press 2007) 3.
69 Ellen Nakashima and Andrea Peterson, 'Obama Faces Growing Momentum to Support Widespread Encryption' *The Washington Post* (Washington, 16 September 2015 <www.washingtonpost.com/world/national-security/tech-trade-agencies-push-to-disavow-

'keeping our options open for such a situation'.[70] Interestingly, US Senator Richard Burr looked beyond the US when he described the November 2015 terrorist attacks in Paris as a 'wake-up call' for encryption.[71] While there was significant speculation about the importance of encryption in the planning of the Paris attacks, it was clear that French law enforcement were far from 'in the dark'. Several of the perpetrators were known to the authorities and evidence emerged after the attack showing that some of the organisers had used standard SMS messaging to communicate.[72] Other information indicates that it was the use of a much simpler technology – prepaid throwaway phones – that assisted the Paris attackers in planning their actions.[73] Inconvenient evidence does not always prevent those in authority from pursuing enhanced powers and such opportunism is not a new phenomenon. Similar calls for legislation have been made following other attacks – most notably including the San Bernardino attacks and the associated Apple v FBI saga – yet the US has yet to successfully legislate to restrict encryption. The debate, and the rhetoric, rumbles on. In spite of obtaining the ability to issue TCNs under the IPA, the UK authorities have continued to make

law-requiring-decryption-of-phones/2015/09/16/1fca5f72-5adf-11e5-b38e-06883aacba 64_story.html>

70 Ellen Nakashima and Andrea Peterson, 'Obama Faces Growing Momentum to Support Widespread Encryption' *The Washington Post* (Washington, 16 September 2015) <www. washingtonpost.com/world/national-security/tech-trade-agencies-push-to-disavow-law-requiring-decryption-of-phones/2015/09/16/1fca5f72-5adf-11e5-b38e-06883aacba64_ story.html>. This statement confirmed what many outside experts had already suspected. Back in April 2015, Michael Vatis opined that there was 'zero chance' of any domestic restrictions on encryption in the US 'absent a catastrophic event which clearly could have been stopped if the government had been able to break some encryption'. Ellen Nakashima and Barton Gellman, 'As Encryption Technology Spreads, US Spies and Law Enforcement Worry About Access to Data for Investigations' *The Washington Post* (Washington, 11 April 2015) <news.nationalpost.com/news/us-encryption-law-enforcemen-739351>

71 Brendan Sasso, 'Senators Take Aim at Encryption in Wake of Paris Attacks' *The Atlantic* (Boston, 17 November 2015) <www.theatlantic.com/politics/archive/2015/11/senators-take-aim-at-encryption-in-wake-of-paris-attacks/457494/>; Ellen Nakashima, 'Officials Seizing the Moment of Paris Attacks to Rekindle Encryption Debate' *The Washington Post* (Washington, 18 November 2015) <www.washingtonpost.com/world/national-security/ officials-seizing-the-moment-of-paris-attacks-to-rekindle-encryption-debate/2015/11/18/ cdb89400-8d5c-11e5-acff-673ae92ddd2b_story.html>

72 Karl Bode, 'After Endless Demonization of Encryption, Police Find Paris Attackers Coordinated via Unencrypted SMS' (*TechDirt*, 18 November 2015) <www.techdirt.com/ articles/20151118/08474732854/after-endless-demonization-encryption-police-find-paris-attackers-coordinated-via-unencrypted-sms.shtml>

73 Glynn Moody, 'Paris Terrorists Used Burner Phones, not Encryption, to Evade Detection' (*Ars Technica*, 21 March 2016) <arstechnica.com/tech-policy/2016/03/paris-terrorist-attacks-burner-phones-not-encryption/>

public calls for action against encryption in the wake of terrorist attacks. For example, May has called for voluntary cooperation from the messaging platform, Telegram, on the basis that 'smaller platforms can quickly become home to criminals and terrorists'.[74] As security analyst Bruce Schneier has written, focusing on the worst possible outcome 'substitutes imagination for thinking, speculation for risk analysis, and fear for reason'.[75] The use of extremist narratives about the security threats a society may face is a particularly powerful rhetorical tool when paired with knowledge inequality. Where evidence for the existential threat is classified, the public has little alternative but to trust those in power.

Encryption and expression – holding power to account

It is clear that encryption has a crucial structural role to play in modern democratic societies. In the digitised world, the sheer amount and richness of data generated makes the innermost thoughts and private actions of each individual more accessible than at any other point in history. As a result, encryption is an essential tool for those who need to ensure a zone of privacy in order to securely communicate.[76] In a democratic society, individuals need to be able to meet, discuss, and develop without fear of undue government interference.[77] Accordingly, in addition to being an important tool for the protection of privacy, the practice of encrypting information in order to send and receive information without government interference also receives protection under Article 19 of the International Covenant on Civil and Political Rights and Article 10 of the European Convention on Human Rights.[78]

74 Alex Hern, 'May Calls Again for Tech Firms to Act on Encrypted Messaging' *The Guardian* (London, 25 January 2018) <www.theguardian.com/technology/2018/jan/25/theresa-may-calls-tech-firms-act-encrypted-messaging>

75 Bruce Schneier, 'Worst-Case Thinking' *(Schneier on Security*, 13 May) <www.schneier.com/blog/archives/2010/05/worst-casethin.html>

76 UNHRC, Twenty Ninth Session 25 May 2015 'Report of the Special Rapporteur on the Promotion and Protection of the Right to Freedom of Opinion and Expression, David Kaye'. UN Doc A/HRC/29/32.

77 For an example of how the chilling effect may influence the activities of individuals see Jonathan Penney, 'Chilling Effects: Online Surveillance and Wikipedia Use' (2016) 31(1) *Berkeley Technology Law Journal* 117.

78 UNHRC, Twenty Ninth Session 25 May 2015 'Report of the Special Rapporteur on the Promotion and Protection of the Right to Freedom of Opinion and Expression, David Kaye'. UN Doc A/HRC/29/32; Maria Helen Murphy, 'Technological Solutions to Privacy Questions: What Is the Role of Law?' (2016) 25(1) *Information & Communications Technology Law* 4–31.

Beyond the individual right to freedom of expression, freedom of the press has long been seen as an essential check on government power in the form of the 'fourth estate'.[79] Encryption is an essential tool for the modern journalist – particularly if the journalist is investigating wrongdoing committed by those in positions of power. Moreover, if there is a perception of a risk that journalistic sources can be easily exposed, a chilling effect will result. As democracies often rely on the press to act as the final outlet for those who wish to report on government malfeasance or illegality, the protection of sources is an essential element of government accountability. This logic also extends to civil society who play a crucial role in democratic societies by channelling the voices of the public to the debate.[80] There is evidence that think tanks and lobbying groups 'viewed as likely to shape future US policies' were targeted by cyber attacks during the 2016 Presidential election. Accordingly, limiting encryption creates security risks that, if exploited, could have significant distorting effects on the democratic process. As the stakes are high, it may not be surprising that law enforcement agencies and government supporters utilise the tools of rhetoric and oversimplification to further their position. For the reasons discussed in this chapter, however, it is vitally important that the implications of restricting encryption for human rights and democracy are made clear and that existing protections are not undermined in a manner veiled from public view.

79 Bollinger goes so far as to state that the 'government is untrustworthy when it comes to regulating public debate, for it will forever try to recapture its authoritarian powers'. Lee Bollinger, *Images of a Free Press* (The University of Chicago Press 1991) 20; Victoria Baranetsky, 'Encryption and the Press Clause' (2017) 6(2) *The New York University Journal of Intellectual Property and Entertainment Law* 179.
80 Susan Landau, *Listening In: Cybersecurity in an Insecure Age* (Yale University Press 2017) 163; Robert Putnam, *Making Democracy Work* (Princeton University Press 1993).

2 Evolving technological standards, same basic rights

The case of the Fourth Amendment

The power-limiting purpose of the Fourth Amendment

A rich source of interpretive debate in the surveillance context has been the Fourth Amendment of the US Constitution and the associated 'third-party doctrine'. The Fourth Amendment affirms:

> The right of the people to be secure in their persons, houses, papers, and effects, against unreasonable searches and seizures, shall not be violated, and no Warrants shall issue, but upon probable cause, supported by Oath or affirmation, and particularly describing the place to be searched, and the persons or things to be seized.

The Fourth Amendment limits executive power by requiring the following of 'certain "judicial processes" to curb executive overreach'.[1] According to the US Supreme Court, two basic guideposts are that the Fourth Amendment seeks to secure 'the privacies of life' against 'arbitrary power' and 'to place obstacles in the way of a too permeating police surveillance'.[2]

The Fourth Amendment is traditionally read to require the obtaining of a warrant on the basis of probable cause from a neutral and detached person before a search can take place. These procedural requirements have been described as not only serving to protect individual liberties, but also as sending 'a message to the executive branch that no person or entity, including those

---

1 Walter Mondale, Robert Stein, and Caitlinrose Fisher, 'No Longer a Neutral Magistrate: The Foreign Intelligence Surveillance Court in the Wake of the War on Terror' (2016) 100(6) *Minnesota Law Review* 2251.
2 *Carpenter v United States* 585 US (2018) 6 citing *Boyd v United States* 116 US 616 (1886) 630 and *United States v Di Re* 332 US 581 (1948) 595.

wielding the most power in society' is 'above the law'.[3] There are circumstances where a warrantless search may not be considered 'unreasonable', however, such as when the search is subsequent to an arrest, in hot pursuit, or in a foreign country.[4]

Debates on the Fourth Amendment have often centred on questions of what constitutes a 'search'.[5] Throughout history, the true meaning of this term has had to be considered in light of technological development and the tangled nature of the question is demonstrated by the recent ruling of the US Supreme Court in the case of *Carpenter v United States*.[6] While the Fourth Amendment was initially interpreted with the protection of private property as the guiding rationale,[7] the case of *Katz v United States* represented an important evolution in interpretation where it was found that the Fourth Amendment 'protects people, not places'.[8] This understanding led to the creation of a technology neutral standard of protection known as the 'reasonable expectation of privacy'.[9]

The third-party doctrine and technological development

While the decision in *Katz v United States* demonstrated the capacity of the Supreme Court to respond to new conditions, the adoption of the 'reasonable expectation of privacy' test left the door open for varied interpretations of where the line should be drawn. The third-party doctrine finds its origin in the case of *United States v Miller* where the Supreme Court held that a person has no 'legitimate expectation of privacy' in information he or she voluntarily provides to third parties.[10] According to the Court, when a person shares

---

3 Walter Mondale, Robert Stein, and Caitlinrose Fisher, 'No Longer a Neutral Magistrate: The Foreign Intelligence Surveillance Court in the Wake of the War on Terror' (2016) 100(6) *Minnesota Law Review* 2251.
4 See HL Pohlman, *Terrorism and the Constitution* (Rowman & Littlefield, New York 2007) 18.
5 Other terms in the Fourth Amendment have also led to debates, such as the scope of the terms 'papers' and 'effects'.
6 *Carpenter v United States* 585 US (2018).
7 Requiring a physical intrusion in order to constitute a Fourth Amendment search. *Olmstead v United States* 277 US 438 (1928).
8 *Katz v United States* 389 US 347 (1967).
9 In spite of this, it should be noted that several of the justices on the Supreme Court tend to turn 'to definitions of place and physical intrusion, particularly when grappling with the challenging privacy issues raised by the constant march of technology'. April Otterberg, 'GPS Tracking Technology: The Case for Revisiting Knotts and Shifting the Supreme Court's Theory of the Public Space Under the Fourth Amendment' (2005) 46(3) *Boston College Law Review* 661. See *United States v Jones* 565 US (2012).
10 *United States v Miller* 425 US 435 (1976) 442–444. Miller had objected to the use of his bank records in a criminal case against him.

information with a third party they take 'the risk . . . that the information will be conveyed by that person to the Government'.[11] In *Smith v Maryland*, the Supreme Court applied the third-party doctrine in the surveillance context. The Supreme Court found that the installation of a 'pen register' on a telephone company's property in order to record the numbers a particular individual dialled on their telephone did not constitute a 'search' for the purposes of the Fourth Amendment.[12] The Supreme Court did not believe that an 'expectation of privacy' existed in telephone numbers dialled as

> [a]ll telephone users realize that they must 'convey' phone numbers to the telephone company, since it is through telephone company switching equipment that their calls are completed. All subscribers realize, moreover, that the phone company has facilities for making permanent records of the numbers they dial.[13]

Strong dissenting judgments were delivered in the case emphasising the absence of choice and how 'unless a person is prepared to forgo use of what for many has become a personal or professional necessity, he cannot help but accept the risk of surveillance'.[14] While Justices Marshall, Brennan, and Stewart showed foresight in this case, the inappropriateness of the third-party doctrine in the communications surveillance context only became clearer with subsequent technological developments.

The difficulty of applying the Fourth Amendment is recognised by Bernal, who notes that the interpretation of the constitutional standard in relation to the internet is complex and 'each new situation seems to call upon a new interpretation'.[15] While the Supreme Court held in *Riley v California*[16] that the search of a mobile phone and the seizure of its digital contents during an arrest required a warrant in order to be constitutional, the decision skirted the question of whether the search of the phone's contents on a service provider's cloud server would require the same protection.[17] Similarly, in the case of *United*

---

11   *United States v Miller* 425 US 435 (1976) 443.

12   *Smith v Maryland* 442 US 735 (1979) 745–746.

13   *Smith v Maryland* 442 US 735 (1979)745–746, 742.

14   *Smith v Maryland* 442 US 735 (1979) Marshall, J, dissenting.

15   Paul Bernal, *Internet Privacy Rights: Rights to Protect Autonomy* (Cambridge University Press 2014) 113–114.

16   It is notable that the Supreme Court in *Riley v California* recognised that the rationales of the rule permitting warrantless searches on arrest had little force when applied to the vast store of sensitive information on a cell phone. *Riley v California* 573 US (2014) 9.

17   The Court stated that because 'the United States and California agree that these cases involve searches incident to arrest, these cases do not implicate the question whether the

States v Jones, the Supreme Court found that interference with an individual's vehicle in order to plant a GPS tracking device constituted a search under the Fourth Amendment, but the majority opinion did not consider whether accessing information communicated via connected GPS tracking devices – including smart phones – would trigger the warrant requirement.[18] While these rulings were narrowly tailored to resolve the facts of the cases before the courts, it left the question of the third-party doctrine unresolved in the digital age.

Considering the amount of data now shared on an almost automatic basis with third parties – from cloud services to internet service providers – it is clear to see how questions may be raised about the application of the third-party doctrine in the modern context. As pointed out in the famous concurring opinion of Justice Sotomayor in *United States v Jones*, the third-party doctrine is 'ill suited to the digital age, in which people reveal a great deal of information about themselves to third parties in the course of carrying out mundane tasks'.[19] The third-party doctrine illustrates how court developed standards can struggle to retain coherence within an ever-evolving technological context. Moreover, the importance of interpretation – and the motives that underlie interpretation – again makes itself clear. As argued in an amici curiae brief in support of the petitioner in *Carpenter v United States*, the notion that an individual voluntarily gives records to telephone companies 'in any realistic sense of the word' seems fanciful.[20]

In the June 2018 decision of the Supreme Court in *Carpenter v United States*, significant steps were made to recognise how the changing technological environment requires the existence of a 'living constitution'.[21] To briefly provide the legal background for the case, under the Stored Communications Act (SCA),[22] government entities can 'require a provider of an electronic communication service or remote computing service to disclose a record or other information pertaining to a subscriber to or customer of such service'.[23] In order to obtain records under the SCA, the government

---

collection or inspection of aggregated digital information amounts to a search under other circumstances'. *Riley v California* 573 US (2014) 19–20.

18 *United States v Jones* 565 US (2012).

19 *United States v Jones* 565 US (2012) Sotomayor, J, concurring, 5.

20 Brief of Amici Curiae Electronic Frontier Foundation, Brennan Center for Justice, The Constitution Project, National Association of Criminal Defense Lawyers, and National Association of Federal Defenders in Support of Petitioner, 19 <www.eff.org/document/amicus-brief-carpenter>

21 *Carpenter v United States* 585 US (2018).

22 SCA 18 USC 2703.

23 SCA 18 USC 2703(c)(d). *Carpenter v United States* 585 US (2018) 10–11.

applicant must obtain either a warrant, a court order, or the consent of the subscriber or customer.[24] Instead of requiring 'probable cause' – which is necessary for the granting of a warrant – a court order compelling disclosure can be issued if the government entity meets the lower standard of offering 'specific and articulable facts showing that there are reasonable grounds to believe that the contents of a wire or electronic communication, or the records or other information sought, are relevant and material to an ongoing criminal investigation'.[25]

In the facts examined in *Carpenter v United States*, the SCA was used by the FBI to compel the disclosure of cell site location information (CSLI) associated with Timothy Carpenter's phone. As time-stamped CSLI is generated every time a mobile phone connects to a 'cell site',[26] the information can be used to track the location of an individual over time. In Carpenter's case, the FBI was able to obtain 12,898 location points that catalogued Carpenter's movements over 127 days. Carpenter objected to the use of this data in his criminal trial on the grounds that a Fourth Amendment search had occurred and a warrant should have been obtained. The evidence was admitted and Carpenter was convicted. On appeal, the US Court of Appeals for the Sixth Circuit applied the third-party doctrine and found that there was no reasonable expectation of privacy in the CSLI as Carpenter had shared it with the service providers as a means of establishing communication.

In overruling the decision of the Sixth Circuit, the majority of the Supreme Court acknowledged how rights must be read in recognition of the current context.[27] Much of the language of the majority opinion recognised how constitutional protections must respond to technological changes if government powers are to be adequately circumscribed. According to Kerr, this has been a theme of Fourth Amendment jurisprudence where courts respond to 'changing technology and social practice' by 'adjusting legal rules to restore the pre-existing balance of police power'. According to Kerr's theory of 'equilibrium-adjustment', when technological developments expand police power, courts can 'tighten Fourth Amendment rules to restore the status quo'.[28] In *Carpenter v United States*, the Supreme Court was mindful to ensure that

---

24 SCA 18 USC 2703(c)(d). SCA 18 USC 2703(c)(1) excludes the disclosure of content data.
25 SCA 18 USC 2703(d).
26 This information is collected and stored by service providers for business purposes.
27 Justices Ginsburg, Breyer, Sotomayor, and Kagan joined the majority opinion of Chief Justice Roberts. Justices Kennedy, Thomas, and Gorsuch each filed a dissenting opinion.
28 Kerr notes that the converse is also true. Orin Kerr, 'An Equilibrium-Adjustment Theory of the Fourth Amendment' (2011) 125(2) *Harvard Law Review* 476.

the Fourth Amendment can place the necessary limitations on government power. Writing for the majority, Chief Justice Roberts recognised that

> the Court is obligated – as '[s]ubtler and more far-reaching means of invading privacy have become available to the Government' – to ensure that the 'progress of science' does not erode Fourth Amendment protections. Here the progress of science has afforded law enforcement a powerful new tool to carry out its important responsibilities. At the same time, this tool risks Government encroachment of the sort the Framers, 'after consulting the lessons of history' drafted the Fourth Amendment to prevent.[29]

It should be noted that in finding that an individual maintains a legitimate expectation of privacy in the 'record of his physical movements as captured through CSLI', the Supreme Court also restricted its holding to the narrow facts of the case. The Supreme Court chose not to decide whether there is a limited period for which the Government may obtain an individual's historical CSLI 'free from Fourth Amendment scrutiny' and limited its main finding to declaring that access to seven days of CSLI constitutes a Fourth Amendment search'.[30]

Furthermore, the Supreme Court did not overrule the third-party doctrine and opted to distinguish *United States v Miller* and *Smith v Maryland* on the grounds that 'bank records' and 'telephone numbers' are in a 'qualitatively different' category to cell site records.[31] Indeed the Court stated that 'CSLI is an entirely different species of business record – something that implicates basic Fourth Amendment concerns about arbitrary government power much more directly than corporate tax or payroll ledgers'.[32] While the Supreme Court decided to distinguish the cases, there is clear potential to see how the logic of the ruling in *Carpenter v United States* could be extended to other – non-location based – categories of information that are conveyed to telecommunications and internet service providers in a future case with different facts. Take for example, the statement of Supreme Court that 'the timestamped data provides an intimate window into a person's life', revealing not only his particular movements, but through them his 'familial,

29 *Carpenter v United States* 585 US (2018) 22. Citing the dissenting opinion of Justice Brandeis in *Olmstead v United States* 277 US 438 (1928) 473–474 and the decision of the Supreme Court (delivered by Justice Jackson) in *United States v Di Re* 332 US 581 (1948) 585.
30 *Carpenter v United States* 585 US (2018) 12.
31 *Carpenter v United States* 585 US (2018) 11, 15–16.
32 *Carpenter v United States* 585 US (2018) 11, 20.

political, professional, religious, and sexual associations'.[33] It is submitted that many other types of 'record data' – including, indeed, records of incoming and outgoing telephone calls – provide an equally intimate window into the life and associations of an individual.[34] In a further narrowing of their holding, the majority also declined to express a view on whether 'real-time CSLI' or 'tower dumps' require a warrant.[35]

The Supreme Court justified its narrow ruling on the grounds that it did not wish to 'embarrass the future'.[36] While there are valid reasons for deciding a case on the facts presented, the decision to avoid a definitive determination on the broader issues in *Carpenter v United States* – as were also avoided in *California v Riley* and *United States v Jones* – leaves a number of important matters unresolved. As a result, it remains a live question as to how the *Carpenter v United States* ruling will play out on the ground. In order to ensure that laws are applied appropriately and consistently in practice, 'bright-line rules' that can be clearly applied by law enforcement are preferable. Consistency and clarity will be compromised where decisions are based on the specific operations of specific technologies.[37] It seems likely that the logic of *Carpenter v United States* will extend to many other contexts, but the avoidance of doubt over whether a warrant will be required for access to non-location data, 'real-time CSLI', 'tower dumps', and records under seven days would have provided much needed clarity for citizens, law enforcement, and lower courts.

Translating judicial standards on the ground

While constitutional standards may sometimes be readily applicable by those tasked to execute the law, it will often be necessary for the legislative branch to 'translate' those standards into a workable set of procedures. Such

---

33 *Carpenter v United States* 585 US (2018) 12, citing *United States v Jones* 565 US (2012) Sotomayor, J, concurring, 3.

34 Though see the Supreme Court's citation of *Riley v California* 573 US (2014) 24 in *Carpenter v United States* 585 US (2018) 16.

35 *Carpenter v United States* 585 US (2018) 17–18. A 'tower dump' is where all the information from all devices connected to a particular cell site are downloaded during a particular interval.

36 It should be noted that the majority did adopt the rule from *Kyllo v United States* that 'more sophisticated systems that are already in use or in development' must be taken into account and according to the majority the 'accuracy of CSLI is rapidly approaching GPS-level precision'. *Carpenter v United States* 585 US (2018) 2–3; *Kyllo v United States* 533 US 27 (2001) 36. Improvements in methods of triangulation and the proliferation of cell sites have greatly increased the accuracy of CSLI, *Carpenter v United States* 585 US (2018) 14–15.

37 Justin Hill, 'Digital Technology and Analog Law: Cellular Location Data, the Third-Party Doctrine, and the Law's Need to Evolve' (2017) 51(3) *University of Richmond Law Review* 773.

legislation is not only important for the clarity and foreseeability it provides the citizen, but also for the certainty it provides to law enforcement who may desire additional guidance. By passing the SCA, Congress has specifically legislated to provide a statutory framework for law enforcement access to electronic information held by third-party service providers. It is notable that in the Sixth Circuit opinion that preceded *Carpenter v United States*, it was remarked that the SCA 'stakes out a middle ground between full Fourth Amendment protection and no protection at all'.[38]

When discussing the SCA, the Sixth Circuit Court of Appeal pointed out that

> one might say that society itself – in the form of its elected representatives in Congress – has already struck a balance that it thinks reasonable. That is not to say that courts should defer to Congress's judgment on constitutional questions. But when the question itself turns on society's views, and society has in a meaningful way already expressed them, judges should bring a certain humility to the task of deciding whether those views are reasonable – lest judges 'confuse their own expectations of privacy,'[39] with those that every reasonable person must hold.[40]

While this is – in the abstract – a compelling account of how the 'reasonable expectation of privacy' may be determined, Hill points out that the SCA was passed in 1986, and so this balance was struck before mobile phone usage was widespread.[41] The outdatedness of the SCA provides an example of the legislative branch failing to keep up with technological change. As seen in *Carpenter v United States*, in such a situation the courts will be required to step in and ensure that the appropriate balance between government power and civil liberty is being struck. When the courts are relied upon to carry out such a complex task, however, far more scope remains for differences of interpretation than in the case of a prospectively designed piece of comprehensive legislation. Interpretive challenges are heightened when accurate interpretation requires both a strong technological knowledge and an understanding of how technological developments may cause new harm to privacy rights.

The pliability of the Fourth Amendment standard is evidenced by the debate over CSLI in recent years. While the Supreme Court has clarified

---

38 *Carpenter v United States* 819 F3d, 889 (discussing *Riley v California* 573 US (2014)).
39 Citing *United States v Jones* 565 US (2012) Alito, J, concurring, 10.
40 *Carpenter v United States* 819 F3d, 890.
41 Justin Hill, 'Digital Technology and Analog Law: Cellular Location Data, the Third-Party Doctrine, and the Law's Need to Evolve' (2017) 51(3) *University of Richmond Law Review* 773.

that CSLI access – at least over seven days – constitutes a Fourth Amendment search, both state and federal courts have reached varying conclusions on the question.[42] In spite of the reasoning under *Carpenter v United States* opening a path for further expansion, the narrow nature of the ruling will undoubtedly lead to further contestation regarding the boundaries of what constitutes a Fourth Amendment search. In addition to the courts having to incorporate the opinion in *Carpenter v United States* into their Fourth Amendment calculations, law enforcement will also have to consider the implications of the ruling for their activities.

An interesting example of the interaction between judicial interpretation and law enforcement interpretation is provided in the 2015 case of *State of North Carolina v Perry*.[43] In this Court of Appeals of North Carolina case, a defendant was appealing a serious drug trafficking conviction. While the police had used cell phone tower records they received from AT&T in the investigation,[44] there is a notable distinction between the facts in *State of North Carolina v Perry* and *Carpenter v United States*.[45] In addition to accessing the historical CSLI that the telephone company (AT&T) held on Paul Perry, the police effectively enlisted AT&T in order to prospectively track the suspect. Rather than giving the investigators the relevant records following a valid request, AT&T emailed the police on an ongoing basis with the location of the cell phone tower 'hits' at 15-minute intervals.[46] The distinction is relevant as several federal courts had found that the SCA only provides a legal basis for the accessing of 'historical' as opposed to 'real-time' location information.[47] Accordingly, the appropriateness of the police relying on the SCA as a legal basis rested on the construed meaning of 'historical' as opposed to 'real time' records.[48]

42 Compare *In re Application of the United States for Historical Cell Site Data* 724 F3d 600 with *United States v Graham* 796 F3d 332 (4th Cir 2015). At the state level, compare *In re Application of the United States for an Order Authorizing the Release of Historical Cell-Site Information* 809 F Supp 2d 113 and *United States v Banks* 52 F Supp 3d 1201 (noting that state Constitutions will also often be relevant).
43 *State of North Carolina v Perry* 776 SE2d 528 (NC Ct App 2015).
44 Similarly to the facts in *Carpenter v United States*, the police in *State of North Carolina v Perry* asserted that no warrant was required due to the third-party rule and reliance on the SCA.
45 Latitudinal and longitudinal coordinates of the cell towers that the defendant's cell phone 'pinged'.
46 The detective testified that 'the hits can range from. . . [a] five or seven meter hit to a couple hundred meter hit'. *State of North Carolina v Perry* 776 SE2d 528 (NC Ct App 2015) 3–4.
47 *United States v Espudo* 954 F Supp 2d 1029, 1034–35 (SD Cal 2013).
48 The Court of Appeals of North Carolina referred to *In Re Application of US for Historical Cell Site Data* 724 F 3d 600, 615 (5th Cir 2013) 12 'holding the receipt of cell site location information under the SCA does not categorically violate the Fourth Amendment as to historical information, but expressly limiting this holding to historical information only'. *In Re*

According to the Detective investigating the case, the records obtained were 'historical hits' as they were not active or 'right on time' and there was 'probably a five- or seven-minute delay' between the time the phone 'pinged' a cell phone tower and the time AT&T calculated the location.[49] The Court agreed and found the access to be valid.[50] The characterisation of a 'five- or seven-minute delay' as rendering a record 'historical' seems open for question and again illustrates the particular importance of interpretation when examining technical applications of the law. Even a concurring judge to the opinion – Chief Judge McGee – took issue with the depiction of the information obtained as 'historical' rather than 'real-time'.[51] To clarify, Chief Judge McGee pointed out that

> '[r]eal time' cell site information refers to data used by the government to identify the location of a phone at the present moment. . . [and] refers to all cell site information that is generated after the government has received court permission to acquire it.[52]

Chief Judge McGee pointed out that the term 'historical cell site location data', as commonly used,

> refers to the acquisition of cell site data for a period retrospective to the date of the order, whereas 'prospective' or 'real-time' cell site data refers [to] the acquisition of data for a period of time *going forward from* the date of the order.[53]

Crucially, the judge pointed out that adopting the majority's characterisation of the information collected would 'obliterate' the vital legal distinction between 'historical' and 'real-time' cell site information.[54]

Now that the Supreme Court has ruled in *Carpenter v United States*, it is clear that access to CSLI over seven days will be considered a Fourth Amendment search. It is notable that the Supreme Court declined to determine whether 'real-time' CSLI was covered by their ruling. It is particularly interesting when one considers that the SCA appears to consider 'real-time' access or tracking to

---

Application of US for Order Directing a Provider of Elec Commc'n Serv to Disclose Records to Gov't 620 F 3d 304, 307–08 (3rd Cir 2010), 'There is no dispute that historical CSLI . . . is a record or other information pertaining to a subscriber'.

49 *State of North Carolina v Perry* 776 SE2d 528 (NC Ct App 2015) 14.

50 *State of North Carolina v Perry* 776 SE2d 528 (NC Ct App 2015) 14.

51 *State of North Carolina v Perry* 776 SE2d 528 (NC Ct App 2015) 3 (dissent).

52 *State of North Carolina v Perry* 776 SE2d 528 (NC Ct App 2015) 5 (dissent). Citing *Maryland Cell Site Case* 402 F Supp 2d 599.

53 *State of North Carolina v Perry* 776 SE2d 528 (NC Ct App 2015) 4 (dissent).

54 *State of North Carolina v Perry* 776 SE2d 528 (NC Ct App 2015) 8 (dissent).

be more intrusive than access to historical data. The majority opinion in *Carpenter v United States* appears to take a different perspective highlighting that

> the retrospective quality of the data here gives police access to a category of information otherwise unknowable. In the past, attempts to reconstruct a person's movements were limited by a dearth of records and the frailties of recollection. With access to CSLI, the Government can now *travel back in time* to retrace a person's whereabouts, subject only to the retention policies of the wireless carriers, which currently maintain records for up to five years. Critically, because location information is continually logged for all of the 400 million devices in the United States – not just those belonging to persons who might happen to come under investigation – this newfound tracking capacity runs against everyone.[55]

The use of the language 'travel back in time' is particularly noteworthy as it draws on the metaphor employed at oral argument by Nathan Wessler arguing on behalf of Timothy Carpenter that

> although police could have gathered a limited set or span of past locations traditionally by canvassing witnesses, for example, never has the government had this kind of a time machine that allows them to aggregate a long period of people's movements over time.[56]

The effective deployment of the metaphor as a means of thinking about the issue illustrates how central language can be in the determination of rights, particularly when technological development requires the reconceptualisation of existing boundaries.

---

55 *Carpenter v United States* 585 US (2018) 13 (emphasis added); Strahilevitz and Tokson also point out how this reasoning is in further tension with the structure of the SCA. Lior Strahilevitz and Matthew Tokson, 'Ten Thoughts on Today's Blockbuster Fourth Amendment Decision – Carpenter v. United States' (*Concurring Opinions*, 22 June 2018) <https://concurringopinions.com/archives/2018/06/ten-thoughts-on-todays-blockbuster-fourth-amendment-decision-carpenter-v-united-states.html>

56 Oral arguments in *Carpenter v United States*, 12 <www.supremecourt.gov/oral_arguments/argument_transcripts/2017/16-402_6khn.pdf>. See also Stephen Henderson, 'Fourth Amendment Time Machines (and What They Might Say About Police Body Cameras)' (2016) 18(3) *University of Pennsylvania Journal of Constitutional Law* 933.

Implications inside and outside of the courtroom

While judicial disagreement on the interpretation of a term – such as 'historical records' – cannot be considered startling, the case of *State of North Carolina v Perry* illustrates how interpretation can have a critical impact on how the law is applied. Even though the US Supreme Court has found the practice of accessing historical cell site location data without a warrant to be unconstitutional, a lower standard has been used in many cases, for many years, by investigative agencies. While the US federal exclusionary rule generally prohibits the admission of evidence obtained in violation of a defendant's Fourth Amendment rights, the courts also recognises a 'good-faith' exception where law enforcements acts 'with an objectively reasonable good-faith belief that their conduct is lawful'.[57] In accordance with this rule, it is unlikely that even Timothy Carpenter will benefit from the ruling in his favour in a practical sense. Moreover, in light of the narrow ruling, many types of information access remain in a zone of a-legality. Certainty will only come as authorities opt to test the boundaries and defendants invoke the application of *Carpenter v United States*.

While acknowledging the challenges that the long-term judicial delineation of such standards pose to legal clarity and justice, it is noted that surveillance carried out in the course of criminal investigations can be contested robustly in court and this is reflected in the voluminous case law. Defendants are, in the main, informed of the fact that their communications data was accessed in the course of investigation. Setting aside the risk of 'parallel construction', the greater transparency of the courts and the criminal justice system means that individuals can challenge the interpretation and application of the law. Crucially, civil society and the general public can learn of how statutes and constitutional documents are being interpreted and have an opportunity to express their views – politically and otherwise. The same, unfortunately, cannot typically be said in other spheres, particularly in the context of intelligence surveillance.[58]

---

57 *Davis v United States* 564 US 229 (2011) 2; *United States v Leon* 468 US 897 (1984).

58 On a related point, it should be noted that the majority in *Carpenter* also made clear that the opinion did not consider collection techniques involving foreign affairs or national security, *Carpenter v United States* 585 US (2018) 18.

3   Executive interpretation

'Word games'

It is clear that words are interpretable and may often have more than one possible meaning. Additional precision is generally expected of legal terms as evidenced by the existence of extensive definition sections in much modern legislation.[1] Statutory definitions may at times differ from common usage, but definition sections provide clarity and certainty for the interested party.[2] As demonstrated by the previous chapter, it is not always the legislative branch that sets out the intended meaning of important legal terms. The courts will often be required to fill in the gaps, particularly when dealing with constitutional documents. In the modern administrative state, the executive branch – and agencies within the executive branch – also have a role in setting out important interpretative guidelines relevant to particular areas of competence. While internal rules and guidelines have been common in many areas of government administration, such tools have been particularly important in the national security arena. In an affront to transparency, however, history has shown that internal executive interpretations of key terms adopted in the national security context have often deviated from the generally understood meaning of those terms.

Secrecy is a key feature of surveillance policy and operations that facilitates the adoption of misleading executive interpretations. Where the reality

---

1 Jarrod Shobe, 'Intertemporal Statutory Interpretation and the Evolution of Legislative Drafting' (2014) 114(4) *Columbia Law Review* 807, 829–830; Seán Patrick Dolan and Rónán Kennedy 'A Flood of Light: Comments on the Interpretation Act 2005' (2006) 6(1) *Judicial Studies Institute Journal* 92, 96; Roderick Munday, 'The Common Lawyer's Philosophy of Legislation' (1983) 14 *Rechtstheorie* 191.
2 It has been argued that for every 'precisely worded definition that clarifies a term's application, another equally precisely defined term complicates an understanding of what instances are covered by the term's reach'. Jeanne Frazier Price, 'Wagging, not Barking: Statutory Definitions' (2013) 60 *Cleveland State Law Review* 999, 1023.

of the situation is obscured, the public can be misled about the extent to which 'internal rules protect rights or constrain power'.[3] In fact, internal interpretations may also be used to mislead the judiciary, the legislature, and sometimes even political members of the executive branch. Even where political figures may have reason to suspect that the internal executive definition may not square with the popular understanding, accepting such terms on their face value provides plausible deniability and political cover in the event of the activities subsequently facing unwelcome public scrutiny.

While secrecy is of course a long-standing feature of national security policy,[4] democratic principles generally entitle citizens to access information about the policies and strategies adopted by their governments. Accordingly, many government agencies now provide some indication of the internal standards that they apply and agree to operate in accordance with. In spite of this, however, even where published standards for executive action may be said to have been met, it is possible that those standards may have only been met under 'a classified and secret exception' protected by state secrets laws.[5] Sinnar has highlighted the strategy of borrowing specific legal terms of art (such as the standard of 'reasonable suspicion') by the US executive branch in an effort to persuade outsiders that sufficient restrictions are applied to executive action.[6] By their invocation of 'rule of law tropes', national security officials are able to 'leverage the credibility of constitutional values to insulate their decision making from external review'.[7] This approach can be particularly useful when dealing with time-restricted but law-conscious and influential elites – such as journalists, lawyers, politicians, and even judges. While governments frequently allude to their consideration of constitutional and

---

3 Shirin Sinnar, 'Rule of Law Tropes in National Security' (2016) 129(6) *Harvard Law Review* 1565, 1579.
4 The UK, for example, denied the existence of MI6 until 1994; the NSA was founded in secret and its internal workings only came to light following the extensive investigative efforts of James Bamford. Maria Helen Murphy, 'Transparency and Surveillance: Assessing the Approach of the Investigatory Powers Tribunal in Liberty & Others' (2016) 1 *Public Law* 9, 10; Helen Fenwick, *Civil Liberties and Human Rights* (Cavendish 2002) 649; Laura Donohue, *The Future of Foreign Intelligence: Privacy and Surveillance in a Digital Age* (Oxford University Press 2016) 5; James Bamford, *The Puzzle Palace* (Houghton Mifflin 1982).
5 *Ibrahim v Department of Homeland Security* 62 F Supp 3d 909, 911, 914, 926 (ND Cal 2014). See Shirin Sinnar, 'Rule of Law Tropes in National Security' (2016) 129(6) *Harvard Law Review* 1565, 1567.
6 Shirin Sinnar, 'Rule of Law Tropes in National Security' (2016) 129(6) *Harvard Law Review* 1565, 1568.
7 Shirin Sinnar, 'Rule of Law Tropes in National Security' (2016) 129(6) *Harvard Law Review* 1565, 1568.

international human rights standards in their surveillance practices, where the internal interpretation differs from the prevailing understanding, authentic evaluation of surveillance practices is impossible. While executive interpretation occurs in all areas of government administration, in the clandestine world of surveillance, secret legal interpretations have been common throughout history.[8] The dominant mode of communication today – via the internet – has increasingly been surveilled by means of 'extralegal regulation'.[9]

While the US constitutional system is built on relatively strong separation of powers principles, increases in executive influence have expanded over time.[10] While measures have been taken at various points to address perceived executive overreach, the continuous trend of expansion has led to a significant accretion of power.[11] Notably, the expansion in executive influence is not limited to the authority of the Commander in Chief, but there has also been a significant accumulation of influence by intelligence agencies within the executive branch. These agencies have developed into vast bureaucracies with significant resources and specific internal cultures.[12] In the modern state, executive agencies make many interpretive choices while carrying out their duties. The culture of secrecy that remains central to these agencies enables the adoption of interpretive choices that can be characterised as 'word games'.[13]

Secret definitions of critical terms that diverge from common understanding can undermine traditional accountability mechanisms. This is illustrated well by James Clapper's infamous testimony in a US senatorial hearing where he was interrogated regarding the NSA's surveillance practices by Senator Ron Wyden of the Senate Intelligence Committee.[14] When asked whether the NSA collected 'any type of data at all on millions or hundreds of millions of Americans?', Clapper stated that the NSA did not 'wittingly'

---

8 Félix Tréguer, 'Intelligence Reform and the Snowden Paradox: The Case of France' (2017) 5(1) *Media and Communication* 17, 19.

9 Félix Tréguer, 'Intelligence Reform and the Snowden Paradox: The Case of France' (2017) 5(1) *Media and Communication* 17, 19.

10 Frederick Schwarz, *Unchecked and Unbalanced: Presidential Power in a Time of Terror* (The New Press 2008).

11 Maria Helen Murphy, 'The Pendulum Effect: Comparisons between the Snowden Revelations and the Church Committee. What are the Potential Implications for Europe?' (2014) 23(3) *Information & Communications Technology Law* 192.

12 Dana Priest and William Arkin, *Top Secret America: The Rise of the New American Security State* (Little, Brown and Company 2011); Michael Turner, 'A Distinctive US Intelligence Identity, International Journal of Intelligence and Counterintelligence' (2004) 17(1) *International Journal of Intelligence and Counterintelligence* 42.

13 Bruce Schneier, 'Surveillance by Algorithm' (*Schneier on Security*, 5 March 2014) <www.schneier.com/blog/archives/2014/03/surveillance_by.html>

14 At the time of the hearing, Clapper was serving as the Director of National Intelligence.

collect such information.[15] Following the Snowden revelations, it became clear to the general public – and not just to the privileged security insiders – that the NSA was indeed gathering data on millions of Americans.[16] Defending his answer, Clapper later commented that 'there are honest differences on the semantics of what – when someone says "collection" to me, that has a specific meaning, which may have a different meaning to him'.[17]

It raises serious questions of transparency when these semantic distinctions are founded on documents obscured from public scrutiny. Even where documents are not fully classified, 'constructive secrecy' may also be used to keep citizens in the dark. For example, it may be possible to piece together an obscure government interpretation by examining a variety of sources and making 'inferential leaps'.[18] The steps required to comprehend the interpretation may, however, only become clear to the outsider with the benefit of hindsight. Notably, support for the counterintuitive interpretation of 'collection' used by Clapper could be found in a 1982 procedures manual from the US Department of Defence that stated:

> Information shall be considered as 'collected' only when it has been received for use by an employee of a DoD [Department of Defence] intelligence component in the course of his official duties. Thus, information volunteered to a DoD intelligence component by a cooperating source would be 'collected' under this procedure when an employee of such component officially accepts, in some manner, such information for use within that component.[19]

15 United States Select Committee on Intelligence, Current and Projected National Security Threats to the United States United States Senate Committee Channel <www.senate.gov/isvp/?comm=intel&type=live&filename=intel031213&stt=22:25&dur=135:15>
16 One of the earliest revelations detailed how the NSA had access to millions of telephone records of American citizens. Glenn Greenwald, 'NSA Collecting Phone Records of Millions of Verizon Customers Daily' *The Guardian* (London, 6 June 2013) <www.theguardian.com/world/2013/jun/06/nsa-phone-records-verizon-court-order>
17 Andrea Mitchell, Interview with Director James R. Clapper, 'Office of the Director of National Intelligence' (8 June 2013) <www.dni.gov/index.php/newsroom/speeches-interviews/speeches-interviews-2013/item/874-director-james-r-clapper-interview-with-andrea-mitchell>. It should be noted that Clapper subsequently apologised for what he described as his 'clearly erroneous' response. Dan Roberts and Spencer Ackerman, 'Clapper Under Pressure Despite Apology for "Erroneous" Statements to Congress' *The Guardian* (London, 1 July 2013) <www.theguardian.com/world/2013/jul/01/james-clapper-apology-congress-erroneous-response>
18 Sudha Setty, 'The President's Private Dictionary: How Secret Definitions Undermine Domestic and Transnational Efforts at Executive Branch Accountability' (2017) 24(2) *Indiana Journal of Global Legal Studies* 513, 523.
19 Department of Defense, Procedures Governing the Activities of Department of Defense Intelligence Components that Affect United States Persons DoD 5240 1-R (December

Furthermore, the document stated that data 'acquired by electronic means is "collected" only when it has been processed into intelligible form'.[20] These interpretations of the term 'collect' raise clear problems of foreseeability. While a government may seek to rely on the inclusion of a counterintuitive interpretation within a technically accessible document as a defence against the claim that it has been relying on 'secret law', if it allows 'the dissonance between the publicly understood meaning and the private, legally operative meaning to stand' then, in reality, the government is perpetuating less effective oversight and helping to undermine the rule of law 'all in secret'.[21]

As pointed out by Irion, it is often not possible to infer the 'scope, boundaries, and consequences' of surveillance powers without accessing internal interpretations.[22] In many instances, 'the exact meaning of surveillance authorities remains largely abstract to the public, unless they make headlines that would convey a more accessible account'.[23] It has been suggested that if Senator Wyden had been aware of the 1982 regulatory definition of 'collect', he could have used this knowledge to directly ask Clapper whether the government 'gathers' or 'stores' – as opposed to 'collects' – any data on millions of Americans. Even though the regulatory definition may not have been a secret in the true sense, it was constructively secret as the administration did not volunteer the meaning that it was relying upon.[24]

Considering that Senate Committee Hearings are held up as a crucial accountability mechanism in US law, the ability of an agency head to circumvent

---

1982) 15. <www.aclu.org/files/assets/eo12333/DIA/DoD%20Regulation%205240.1-R,%
20Procedures%20Governing%20the%20Activities%20of%20DoD%20Intelligence%20
Components%20that%20Affect%20United%20States%20Persons.pdf>

20 Department of Defense, Procedures Governing the Activities of Department of Defense Intelligence Components that Affect United States Persons DoD 5240 1-R (December 1982) 15. <www.aclu.org/files/assets/eo12333/DIA/DoD%20Regulation%205240.1-R,%
20Procedures%20Governing%20the%20Activities%20of%20DoD%20Intelligence%20
Components%20that%20Affect%20United%20States%20Persons.pdf>

21 Sudha Setty, 'The President's Private Dictionary: How Secret Definitions Undermine Domestic and Transnational Efforts at Executive Branch Accountability' (2017) 24(2) *Indiana Journal of Global Legal Studies* 513, 523.

22 Kristina Irion, 'Accountability Unchained: Bulk Data Retention, Preemptive Surveillance, and Transatlantic Data Protection' in Marc Rotenberg, Jeramie Scott, and Julia Horowitz (eds), *Privacy in the Modern Age: The Search for Solutions* (The New Press 2015) 1179–1181.

23 Kristina Irion, 'Accountability Unchained: Bulk Data Retention, Preemptive Surveillance, and Transatlantic Data Protection' in Marc Rotenberg, Jeramie Scott, and Julia Horowitz (eds), *Privacy in the Modern Age: The Search for Solutions* (The New Press 2015) 1179–1181.

24 Sudha Setty, 'The President's Private Dictionary: How Secret Definitions Undermine Domestic and Transnational Efforts at Executive Branch Accountability' (2017) 24(2) *Indiana Journal of Global Legal Studies* 513, 536.

that accountability by slight of language demonstrates the weaknesses of the oversight provided. Wyden was asking the question from a position of privileged knowledge but was unable to directly challenge the NSA Director on the obfuscation due to the classified nature of the information that he had obtained through his role on the Senate Intelligence Committee. This is a clear example of how state secrets laws can undermine the effectiveness of oversight. It is the type of loop-hole that might discourage a similar line of questioning from a less-committed senator. The truth of the matter may never have become fully apparent without the Snowden revelations. The transparency-washing nature of the oversight mechanism was acknowledged by Clapper himself when he stated that an 'open hearing on intelligence matters is something of a contradiction in terms'. In spite of this acknowledgement, Clapper asserted that it was 'important to keep the American public informed'.[25] It seems that what constitutes keeping the public 'informed' is also a matter of interpretation.

It has already been shown how the use of a familiar and unthreatening metaphor can be a powerful tool when normalising surveillance measures in the perception of the public.[26] Clapper utilised this rhetorical device by evoking the benign image of a library when he was eventually drawn on the NSA's non-standard definition of 'collection'. He described the data stored by the NSA as akin to a library where many of the books stored on the shelves are never actually read.[27] Relying on this metaphor, Clapper asserted that the 'collection of US Persons data would mean taking the book off the shelf, opening it up and reading it' – not merely obtaining and storing that data. According to Clapper, the important point is that the authorities try to be as precise as they can be when they 'go in that library and look for the books' that they 'need to open up and actually read'. It is an inappropriate choice of metaphor as it is common for book collectors to have many books in their collection that they have not read, yet, precision is not the purpose of the metaphor in this instance. In characterising the obtaining of information on millions of individuals without regard to traditional notions of individualised suspicion in this manner, Clapper attempts to minimise the significance of the surveillance practice for the average citizen. Clapper explains away the fact

---

25 Office of the Director of National Intelligence Public Affairs Office, Remarks as delivered by James R. Clapper, 'Director of National Intelligence Worldwide Threat Assessment to the Senate Select Committee on Intelligence' (12 March 2013) 2 <www.dni.gov/files/documents/Intelligence%20Reports/WWTA%20Remarks%20as%20delivered%2012%20Mar%202013.pdf>
26 See Chapter 1.
27 Andrea Mitchell, Interview with Director James R. Clapper, 'Office of the Director of National Intelligence' (8 June 2013) <www.dni.gov/index.php/newsroom/speeches-interviews/speeches-interviews-2013/item/874-director-james-r-clapper-interview-with-andrea-mitchell>

that data is certainly collected in the ordinary sense of the word by insinuating that it is only the 'reading' or analysing of the data that actually matters. Of course, if that was indeed the case, the rules could have been written to make the situation clear in order to allow a full democratic debate on whether such 'collection' or 'accumulation' should be permitted in the first place.

The non-standard interpretation of 'collection' is, of course, not the only instance of such diverging interpretation in US surveillance practice.[28] Wyden has described the culture of US intelligence agencies as being one of 'misinformation' towards not only adversaries but also towards members of the public and Members of Congress.[29] Indeed, this culture of misinformation has been shown to extend to communications with the Foreign Intelligence Surveillance Court – a court specially designed to oversee the foreign intelligence actions of US government agencies while also taking due regard of operational requirements for secrecy. In the footnote of a subsequently declassified Foreign Intelligence Surveillance Court Memorandum Opinion, Judge John Bates stated that he was 'troubled that the government's revelations regarding NSA's acquisitions of Internet transactions mark the third instance in less than three years in which the government has disclosed a substantial misrepresentation regarding the scope of a major collection program'.[30]

---

28 Such examples are not entirely limited to the surveillance sphere, of course. One scholar has gone so far as to speak of the President's 'private dictionary'. Sudha Setty, 'The President's Private Dictionary: How Secret Definitions Undermine Domestic and Transnational Efforts at Executive Branch Accountability' (2017) 24(2) *Indiana Journal of Global Legal Studies* 513. Infamous examples in the broader national security sphere include the strained interpretations set out in the Torture Memoranda and the international law divergent interpretation of 'imminent' threat adopted by the Obama administration in its use of drones for targeted killings. Memorandum from Jay S. Bybee, Assistant Attorney General, US Department of Justice Office of Legal Counsel, to Alberto R Gonzales, Counsel to the President (1 August 2002); Memorandum from Daniel Levin, Acting Assistant Attorney General, US Department of Justice Office of Legal Counsel, to James B Comey, Deputy Attorney General (30 December 2004). Anna Diakun, 'Fighting to Bring the Drone Program into the Light' (*ACLU*, 25 October 2016) <www.aclu.org/blog/speak-freely/fighting-bring-drone-program-light>. See Sudha Setty, 'No More Secret Laws: How Transparency of Executive Branch Legal Policy Doesn't Let the Terrorists Win' (2009) 57 *University of Kansas Law Review* 579, 589, 591; Sudha Setty, 'The President's Private Dictionary: How Secret Definitions Undermine Domestic and Transnational Efforts at Executive Branch Accountability' (2017) 24(2) *Indiana Journal of Global Legal Studies* 513, 529–533.
29 Peter Gill, 'Should the Intelligence Agencies "Show More Leg" or Have They Just Been Stripped Naked?' (2013) 30 *Information & Security: An International Journal* 11, 22; Spencer Ackerman, 'NSA Guideline Breaches Contradict Assurances from the White House' *The Guardian* (London, 17 August 2013) 20.
30 John D Bates, 'Foreign Intelligence Surveillance Court Memorandum Opinion and Order' (October 2011) 16–17 <www.dni.gov/files/documents/0716/October-2011-Bates-Opinion-and%20Order-20140716.pdf>

As questionable transparency practices have been a feature of surveillance regimes around the world, it is worthwhile to consider what role a human rights analysis might play in setting out the appropriate boundaries and procedures for surveillance operations that fulfil democratic obligations. While states have traditionally been reluctant to accept the legitimacy of human rights critique in the area of national security, and arguments have been made against the inflexible application of human rights in the surveillance context,[31] the global nature of surveillance makes it all the more important that the mutually agreed standards set down in international human rights treaties be considered. It is clear that the misleading practices adopted in the surveillance sphere raise issues under the standards set out in Article 17 of the International Covenant on Civil and Political Rights. Article 17 ICCPR provides that '[e]veryone has the right to the protection of the law' against 'arbitrary or unlawful interference with his privacy'. Accordingly, international human rights law requires that surveillance programmes be governed by publicly accessible law. As pointed out in the Report of the Office of the United Nations High Commissioner for Human Rights on the right to privacy in the digital age

> 'Accessibility' requires not only that the law is published, but that it is sufficiently precise to enable the affected person to regulate his or her conduct, with foresight of the consequences that a given action may entail.[32]

In light of this, 'secret rules and secret interpretations – even secret judicial interpretations – of law do not have the necessary qualities of "law"'.[33] Emphasis on the importance of foreseeability and accessibility has been central to the surveillance jurisprudence of the European Court of Human Rights (ECtHR) for several decades. Due to the direct role the ECtHR has had in influencing the form of surveillance legislation in many European countries – as well as its influence on the increasingly important Court of Justice of the European Union jurisprudence – the next section sets out the key aspects of the case law of the ECtHR that address the question of secret surveillance law.

---

31 Asaf Lubin, '"We Only Spy on Foreigners": The Myth of a Universal Right to Privacy and the Practice of Foreign Mass Surveillance' (2018) 12(2) *Chicago Journal of International Law* 501.
32 UNHCR, Twenty-seventh Session 30 June 2014 'Report of the Office of the United Nations High Commissioner for Human Rights, The Right to Privacy in the Digital Age'. UN Doc A/HRC/27/37, 10.
33 UNHCR, Twenty-seventh Session 30 June 2014 'Report of the Office of the United Nations High Commissioner for Human Rights, The Right to Privacy in the Digital Age'. UN Doc A/HRC/27/37, 10.

Foreseeability and accessibility in the surveillance case law of the European Court of Human Rights

Article 8 of the European Convention on Human Rights (ECHR) guarantees the right to respect for private life. The second paragraph of Article 8 ECHR prohibits interference with the exercise of the right except such as is 'in accordance with the law' and is 'necessary in a democratic society' in the pursuit of a legitimate aim.[34] In contrast to other contexts, when dealing with surveillance cases, the ECtHR has tended to focus its scrutiny on the 'in accordance with the law' or 'legality' test and has placed a strong emphasis on rule of law values.[35] Where rules are secret, individuals will not 'have an indication that is adequate, in the circumstances, of the legal rules applicable to a given case'.[36] In spite of this basic premise, the ECtHR recognises that the requirements of foreseeability 'cannot be exactly the same in the special context of interception of communications'. Nevertheless, in the early surveillance case of *Malone v United Kingdom*, the ECtHR stated that the Government must ensure that the law is sufficiently clear in its terms to give citizens

> an adequate indication as to the circumstances in which and the conditions on which public authorities are empowered to resort to this secret and potentially dangerous interference with the right to respect for private life and correspondence.[37]

While the importance of protecting operational secrecy in the surveillance context is recognised by the ECtHR, the Court has also been alert to the risks of covert activities stating that

> it would be contrary to the rule of law for the discretion granted to the executive or to a judge to be expressed in terms of an unfettered power. Consequently, the law must indicate the scope of any such discretion conferred on the competent authorities and the manner of its exercise

---

34 The legitimate aims set out in Article 8(2) ECHR are where the interference is in the interests of 'national security, public safety or the economic wellbeing of the country, for the prevention of disorder or crime, for the protection of health or morals, or for the protection of the rights and freedoms of others'.

35 Maria Helen Murphy, 'A Shift in the Approach of the European Court of Human Rights in Surveillance Cases: A Rejuvenation of Necessity?' (2014) 5 *European Human Rights Law Review* 507, 511.

36 *Klass and Others v Germany* (1979) 2 EHRR 214, 55.

37 *Malone v UK* (1984) 7 EHRR 14, 67.

with sufficient clarity to give the individual adequate protection against arbitrary interference.[38]

The ECtHR has clarified that surveillance interferences that are classified as 'serious' must be 'based on a "law" that is particularly precise'. In addition to specifying what surveillance measures are permitted, surveillance laws should also specify the circumstances under which surveillance can be conducted. In the case of *Roman Zakharov v Russia*, the Grand Chamber of the ECtHR restated the necessity of setting out the following minimum safeguards in surveillance legislation:

the nature of offences which may give rise to an interception order;
a definition of the categories of people liable to have their telephones tapped;
a limit on the duration of telephone tapping;
the procedure to be followed for examining, using and storing the data obtained;
the precautions to be taken when communicating the data to other parties; and the circumstances in which recordings may or must be erased or destroyed.[39]

While the focus on these 'quality of law' issues can be questioned, the rulings of the ECtHR have certainly catalysed the placing of secret surveillance on a legal basis in many European countries.[40] The integration

---

38 *Roman Zakharov v Russia* [2015] ECHR 1065, 230; *Malone v UK* (1984) 7 EHRR 14, 68; *Weber and Saravia v Germany* [2006] ECHR 1173, 94.
39 Where the surveillance intrusion is considered 'serious' by the ECtHR. This has been held to include individualised interception and generalised surveillance. *Roman Zakharov v Russia* [2015] ECHR 1065, 231.
40 Maria Helen Murphy, 'A Shift in the Approach of the European Court of Human Rights in Surveillance Cases: A Rejuvenation of Necessity?' (2014) 5 *European Human Rights Law Review* 507, 511. For example, Article 100 of the French Code of Criminal Procedure was amended in response to notable judgements in *Huvig v France* (1990) 12 EHRR 528, 32 and *Kruslin v France* (1990) 12 EHRR 547. The surveillance case law also led to interception of communications being put on a legal basis for the first time in Spain: Lorena Winter, 'Telephone Tapping in the Spanish Criminal Procedure: An Analysis from the European Court of Human Rights' Perspective' (2007) *Jura: A Pécsi Tudományegyetem Állam-és Jogtudományi Karának tudományos lapja* 2, 7. <http://jura.ajk.pte.hu/JURA_2007_2. pdf>. The UK has responded to a number of negative judgements with new surveillance laws: Bethan Loftus, Benjamin Goold, and Shane MacGiollabhui, 'Covert Policing and the Regulation of Investigatory Powers Act 2000' (2010) 8 *Archbold Review* 5. More recently, the UK has had to respond to surveillance rulings from the Court of Justice of the European Union and UK surveillance practices are again under review in the European Court

of 'rule of law' supporting safeguards into the legality requirement makes sense when viewed from a practical perspective. The ECtHR clearly acknowledges the culture of secrecy prevalent in surveillance operations and as a result, recognises that simply identifying broad principles and expecting good faith compliance without the check of explicit and transparent safeguards is unlikely to prove effective for the protection of privacy rights.

The principle of legality in practice

In spite of being the first signatory to the ECHR, and indeed, in spite of designing much of its surveillance legislation in direct response to rulings of the ECtHR, it is important to note that similar transparency deficiencies to those discussed in the US context have also been identified in UK surveillance law.[41] Even though the UK has responded to ECtHR rulings on the foreseeability and accessibility of its surveillance rules by promulgating more detailed law on numerous occasions, its efforts have been described as 'minimalist'.[42] Indicating the scale of the transparency problem created by the now partially repealed Regulation of Investigatory Powers Act (RIPA), David Anderson described the law as 'incomprehensible to all but a tiny band of initiates'.[43] The ambiguities of the UK law can be illustrated by considering the interpretation of 'external' communications as used in RIPA. The distinction between 'internal' and 'external' interception was of key significance in the statutory framework that governed UK surveillance before the Investigatory Powers Act entered into force.[44] Under section 8 of RIPA, 'internal' interception was subject to comparatively stringent

---

of Human Rights, *Tele2 Sverige AB v Post-och telestyrelsen and Secretary of State for the Home Department v Tom Watson and Others* [2017] 2 WLR 1289; *10 Human Rights Organisations v The United Kingdom* App no 24960/15 (ECHR).

41 Maria Helen Murphy, 'Transparency and Surveillance: Assessing the Approach of the Investigatory Powers Tribunal in Liberty & Others' (2016) 1 *Public Law* 9, 10–11.

42 Benjamin Goold, 'Liberty and Others v The United Kingdom: A New Chance for Another Missed Opportunity' (2009) *Public Law* 5.

43 Indeed, during a House of Commons Debate on the Report of the Investigatory Powers Review, Dominic Grieve suggested that 'even the initiates sometimes found it incomprehensible'. Hansard, HC vol 597, col 1092 (25 June 2015). David Anderson, *A Question of Trust – Report of the Investigatory Powers Review* (June 2015) <https://terrorismlegislationreviewer. independent.gov.uk/wp-content/uploads/2015/06/IPR-Report-Web-Accessible1.pdf>

44 Jemima Stratford and Tim Johnston, 'The Snowden "Revelations": Is GCHQ Breaking the Law?' (2014) 2 *European Human Rights Law Review* 129, 130.

controls. In particular, section 8 RIPA required the identification of a named person or premises in the warrant for the interception.[45] In contrast, much broader interception warrants were permitted in relation to 'external' communications.[46] While 'internal' interception required tailored warrants, 'external' interception allowed for the bulk collection of communications content.[47] A related question of language concerned the interpretation of the term 'communication'.[48]

Like the 'collection' example discussed above in the US context, the issue with the internal interpretation of the term 'external' only fully came to light following the Snowden revelations.[49] In a witness statement in the *Liberty v GCHQ*[50] case before the Investigatory Powers Tribunal (IPT), Charles Farr[51] clarified that, under the Government's interpretation, a search engine request made by a person in the UK would involve two 'external communications' where the relevant Google web server was located outside the

<hr/>

45 The Regulation of Investigatory Powers Act 2000 (RIPA), s 8(1)–(3).
46 RIPA, s 8(4)–(6). External communications were defined as communications 'sent or received outside the British Islands' RIPA, s 20.
47 Jemima Stratford and Tim Johnston, 'The Snowden "Revelations": Is GCHQ Breaking the Law?' (2014) 2 *European Human Rights Law Review* 129, 131. It should be noted that 'internal' communications may also be intercepted under section 8(5) whereby the 'internal' communications are necessarily intercepted in order to do what is authorised by the warrant, RIPA, ss 5(6) and 8(5)(b).
48 RIPA defines a 'communication' as including 'signals serving either for the impartation of anything between persons, between a person and a thing or between things or for the actuation or control of any apparatus'. RIPA, s 81.
49 The classified documents leaked by Edward Snowden confirmed the scale of the UK surveillance programmes in operation for the first time. Not only had the UK Government been operating a programme that involved the interception of content and communications data passing through submarine fibre optic cables entering and exiting the UK (TEMPORA), but GCHQ also had access to communications as they moved over the internet via major internet cables through agreed access to US surveillance programmes UPSTREAM and PRISM. While the UK government denied the existence of TEMPORA, leaked documents indicate that it has been authorised by a series of generic warrants issued under section 8(4) of RIPA. *10 Human Rights Organisations v The United Kingdom* App no 24960/15 (ECHR) (Additional Submissions on the Facts and Complaints) 5 <www.amnesty.org/download/Documents/IOR6014152015ENGLISH.PDF>
50 *Liberty, Privacy International, American Civil Liberties Union, Amnesty International, and Bytes for All v The Government Communications Headquarters, the Secretary of State for the Foreign and Commonwealth Office, and the Security Service* [2014] UKIPTrib 13_77-H.
51 Of the Office for Security and Counter-Terrorism.

British Islands.[52] Moreover, where a person posted on a social network the 'recipient of the relevant "communication"' would not be 'any particular person who eventually reads the post or tweet'.[53] The relevant recipient, according to Farr, would be the platform itself. Accordingly, where a person located in the British Islands posted a message on a social network website using a web server located outside of the British Islands, the message would be considered an 'external communication'.[54] The surveillance of these 'communications' would, as a result, be subject to the less-strict regime governing 'external' communications.[55] These interpretations were not clear prior to the statement made by Farr in the *Liberty v GCHQ* case, discussed further below, that was itself catalysed by the Snowden revelations.[56] As pointed out by David Anderson, the distinctions drawn in these interpretations could be considered 'counter-intuitive: for example, many people might not consider a Google search to be a communication at all, let alone an external communication'.[57]

52 Witness: Charles Farr Statement Number: 1 Exhibit: CF1 (16 May 2014) 134 <https://blog.bytemark.co.uk/wp-content/uploads/2014/06/witness_st_of_charles_blandford_farr-2.pdf>

53 It should be noted that the technical difficulty of accurately separating factually internal communications (where an individual in the British Islands contacts another individual in the British Islands) from external communications on modern communications networks also raises questions of foreseeability. In the *Liberty* case the IPT stated that it was inevitable that when a telephone call is made from a mobile phone or iPhone, or an email is sent to an email address, it will not necessarily be known whether it will be received in the United Kingdom or in the course of travel or at a foreign destination. *Liberty, Privacy International, American Civil Liberties Union, Amnesty International, and Bytes for All v The Government Communications Headquarters, the Secretary of State for the Foreign and Commonwealth Office, and the Security Service* [2014] UKIPTrib 13_77-H, 94–95.

54 Witness: Charles Farr Statement Number: 1 Exhibit: CF1 Dated: (16 May 2014) 136–137 <https://blog.bytemark.co.uk/wp-content/uploads/2014/06/witness_st_of_charles_blandford_farr-2.pdf>

55 Graham Smith, 'Investigatory Powers Review Written Submissions' (H-V) 222–223 <https://terrorismlegislationreviewer.independent.gov.uk/wp-content/uploads/2015/06/Submissions-H-Z.pdf>

56 *Liberty, Privacy International, American Civil Liberties Union, Amnesty International, and Bytes for All v The Government Communications Headquarters, the Secretary of State for the Foreign and Commonwealth Office, and the Security Service* [2014] UKIPTrib 13_77-H. See also *Liberty & Others v The Secretary of State for Foreign and Commonwealth Affairs & Others* [2015] UKIPTrib 13_77-H.

57 David Anderson, *A Question of Trust – Report of the Investigatory Powers Review* (June 2015) <https://terrorismlegislationreviewer.independent.gov.uk/wp-content/uploads/2015/06/IPR-Report-Web-Accessible1.pdf>. Additional problems with the category of external communications include the incongruity of the concept in the modern global

It is notable that the UK's surveillance court – the IPT – considered the question of whether 'the difficulty of determining the difference between external and internal communications' meant that the surveillance regime did not meet the ECHR 'in accordance with law' standards in the case of *Liberty v GCHQ*.[58] This ruling of the IPT – and subsequent related rulings – considered a number of issues surrounding the bulk collection of communications data and data sharing practices with US intelligence agencies. Efforts at transparency were resisted by the UK government as the applicants sought disclosure of all surveillance policies and guidance adopted by the services. With the Government adopting the position of neither confirming nor denying, the IPT hearing set out to determine issues of law on the basis of 'assumed hypothetical factual premises agreed between the parties'.[59] While the UK Government defended the intelligence gathering practices as being in compliance with existing publicly available law, the implications of those laws and codes only became evident with the release of the Snowden documents.

In a tepid endorsement of the importance of foreseeability, the IPT stated that 'sufficient signposting of the rules or arrangements' governing surveillance measures is required.[60] This interpretation of foreseeability appears to fall short of the standards set out by the ECtHR in its jurisprudence. As pointed out

---

communications context and the fact that it appeared to be practically impossible to intercept external communications without also intercepting internal communications.

58 While a number of issues were raised by the multiple parties to the case, the IPT highlighted four key questions for consideration. In addition to the question regarding the interpretation of 'internal' and 'external', the other three questions were: 'Insofar as s.16 of RIPA is required as a safeguard in order to render the interference with Article 8 in accordance with law, is it a sufficient one?'; 'Is the regime, whether with or without s.16, sufficiently compliant with the *Weber* requirements, insofar as such is necessary in order to be in accordance with law?'; and 'Is s.16(2) indirectly discriminatory contrary to Article 14 of the Convention, and, if so, can it be justified?'. *Liberty v GCHQ* [2014] UKIPTrib 13_77-H, 80; see also *Liberty v GCHQ* [2015] UKIPTrib 13_77-H.

59 In Charles Farr's witness statement it was asserted that the internal arrangements of the intelligence services under sections 15 and 16 RIPA 'cannot safely be put into the public domain without undermining the effectiveness of interception methods' Witness: Charles Farr Statement Number: 1 Exhibit: CF1 (16 May 2014) 100 <https://blog.bytemark.co.uk/wp-content/uploads/2014/06/witness_st_of_charles_blandford_farr-2.pdf>. It was also stated that the arrangements and procedures for US-UK intelligence sharing and processing 'cannot safely be published without undermining the interests of national security and the prevention and detection of serious crime'.

60 Maria Helen Murphy, 'Transparency and Surveillance: Assessing the Approach of the Investigatory Powers Tribunal in Liberty & Others' (2016) 1 *Public Law* 9.

by the '10 Human Rights Organisations' that are challenging the UK regime at the ECtHR, 'signpost' is something that points elsewhere. What Articles 8 and 10 require is that the relevant arrangements are understood by those subject to them, not that those persons are given indications that the understanding is located somewhere else that is inaccessible to the public.[61]

While the IPT acknowledged that technical changes have led to unexpected communications being potentially classed as 'external', the Tribunal found that the difficulties in differentiating the terms were foreseen at the time RIPA was passed by Parliament.[62] While this finding would appear to be beside the point, the IPT found that the use of the terms 'external' and 'internal' did not raise issues under the foreseeability standards of the ECtHR.[63] As the IPT also rejected most of the other complaints raised, it is not surprising that a complaint was subsequently made to the ECtHR. While the complaints raise a number of complex issues, the ambiguous distinction between 'internal' and 'external' communications – and the accompanying differentiated treatment of such communications – is one of the points raised by the complainants. They argue that 'if there is real uncertainty as to which types of internet-based communications are internal and external, then it follows that the scope of s8(4) warrants in relation to "external" communications lacks clarity'.[64]

Beyond legality and the role of the judiciary

In addition to being 'in accordance with the law', interferences with Article 8 ECHR can only be justified where they are 'necessary in a democratic

---

61 *10 Human Rights Organisations v The United Kingdom* App no 24960/15 (ECHR) (Additional Submissions on the Facts and Complaints) 60 <www.amnesty.org/download/Documents/IOR6014152015ENGLISH.PDF>

62 *Liberty v GCHQ* [2014] UKIPTrib 13_77-H, 98–102.

63 The IPT noted that with regard to this question, their answer was given 'with the benefit of the Disclosures by the Respondents' given in the course of the tribunal proceedings. In the second ruling, it was found that prior to the disclosures brought about by IPT proceedings, 'the regime governing the soliciting, receiving, storing and transmitting by UK authorities of private communications of individuals located in the UK, which have been obtained by US authorities pursuant to Prism and/or Upstream, contravened Articles 8 or 10 ECHR'. In light of the disclosure, the IPT found the regime to be in compliance subsequently. As pointed out by Murphy '[t]he inference of this finding is that the "in accordance with the law" deficiencies of the surveillance arrangement were remedied by the transparency effectively imposed on the agencies through the pursuit of legal redress'. Maria Helen Murphy, 'Transparency and Surveillance: Assessing the Approach of the Investigatory Powers Tribunal in Liberty & Others' (2016) 1 *Public Law* 9, 14. *Liberty v GCHQ* [2015] UKIPTrib 13_77-H.

64 *10 Human Rights Organisations v The United Kingdom* App no 24960/15 (ECHR) (Additional Submissions on the Facts and Complaints) 45 <www.amnesty.org/download/Documents/IOR6014152015ENGLISH.PDF>

society' in pursuit of a legitimate aim. As previously mentioned, the ECtHR has typically placed particular emphasis on the 'in accordance with the law' part of the inquiry when considering surveillance cases. Notably, where the ECtHR has considered whether a surveillance measure is 'necessary in a democratic society', the inquiry has also been focused on process as opposed to abstract assessments of 'necessity'.[65] Accordingly, when considering whether a surveillance regime is 'necessary in a democratic society', the ECtHR requires the existence of 'adequate and effective guarantees against abuse'.[66] The key question is whether the procedures for supervising the ordering and implementation of surveillance are such as to keep the 'interference' with Article 8 ECHR to what is 'necessary in a democratic society'. The ECtHR will consider

the nature, scope and duration of the possible measures,
the grounds required for ordering them,
the authorities competent to authorise, carry out and supervise them, and
the kind of remedy provided by the national law.[67]

In addition to providing for some protections that overlap with the legality requirements restated in *Roman Zakharov v Russia*, the process-driven necessity test places significant emphasis on the authorities competent to authorise and supervise surveillance measures and the related provision of remedies in domestic law. While the seminal case of *Klass v Germany* recognised that 'judicial control' offers 'the best guarantees of independence, impartiality and a proper procedure',[68] the ECtHR has placed increased emphasis on the importance of notification and judicial authorisation as surveillance case law has progressed.[69] There has been noted cross-fertilisation of reasoning between the ECtHR case law and the recent surveillance jurisprudence of the Court of Justice of the European Union. In addition to citing the ECtHR case law on surveillance, the CJEU in *Digital Rights Ireland* criticised

---

65 Maria Helen Murphy, 'A Shift in the Approach of the European Court of Human Rights in Surveillance Cases: A Rejuvenation of Necessity?' (2014) 5 *European Human Rights Law Review* 507, 511.
66 *Roman Zakharov v Russia* [2015] ECHR 1065, 232.
67 *Roman Zakharov v Russia* [2015] ECHR 1065, 232.
68 *Klass and Others v Germany* (1979) 2 EHRR 214, 55 and 56.
69 *Roman Zakharov v Russia* [2015] ECHR 1065, 233; Paul de Hert and Franziska Boehm, 'The Rights of Notification after Surveillance is Over: Ready for Recognition?' in Jacques Bus, Malcolm Crompton, Mireille Hildebrandt, and George Metakides (eds), *Digital Enlightenment Yearbook* (IOS Press 2012) 19–39. The recent Third Section case of *Centrum För Rättvisa v Sweden* App no 35252/08 (ECHR, 19 June 2018) may be seen as a step back regarding the connected issues of accessible remedies and notification.

the absence of a requirement for judicial (or independent administrative) authorisation for access to retained data under the Data Retention Directive. According to the CJEU, such authorisation is needed to limit the access and use of such data 'to what is strictly necessary for the purpose of attaining the objective pursued'.[70] In effect, the requirement for an independent review of surveillance measures at the authorisation stage is designed to realise the requirements of 'necessity' and proportionality in practice.

These developments indicate some recognition that simply requiring standards and rules to be set out in law is unlikely to protect rights in practice where actual incidents remain secret and where internal executive bodies interpret and apply the law with minimal independent scrutiny. This is why the emphasis on review and redress has become so important. In light of the trust placed in the judiciary to resolve the accountability conundrum, the following chapter considers the role of the judiciary in the surveillance context.

---

70 *Digital Rights Ireland and Seitlinger and Others* [2014] WLR (D) 164, 62.

4 Independent oversight in the surveillance context

Surveillance courts: opacity and potential for capture

While this book has discussed the interpretive role played by members of the executive branch, in a 'government of laws, not of men', courts often hold the ultimate responsibility for 'stating what the law is'.[1] One of the most important roles of the judiciary is to hold the executive branch to account. As the judiciary is designed to provide an independent check on arbitrary exercises of government power, the role of the judiciary is particularly important where the scope of rights is being determined. Under the understanding that judicial review of executive action is possible, the executive should be deterred from taking arbitrary or abusive action and will be incentivised to take into account constitutional standards in their operations. The judicial check on executive surveillance action will clearly be more effective where there is an established tradition of judicial review and a recognised right to privacy.

Even where such a constitutional system exists, however, the likelihood of excessive deference to executive assertions of competence – while prevalent in many areas – is greatly increased in the surveillance context. This is in part due to the frequent association of surveillance measures with matters of national security and also due to the avowed importance of secrecy in the field. In the US context, Rudenstine has pointed out that if the rule of law is not only to be considered an ideal, but a reality, 'then the courts will need to abandon a posture of acquiescence in favor of shaping legal doctrines that make the executive toe the legal line and respect the rule of law'.[2] A significant obstacle to such an approach being adopted is the degree of secrecy insisted upon by

---

1 David Rudenstine, *The Age of Deference: The Supreme Court, National Security and the Constitutional Order* (Oxford University Press 2016) 315.
2 David Rudenstine, *The Age of Deference: The Supreme Court, National Security and the Constitutional Order* (Oxford University Press 2016) 315.

the executive in this area. This secrecy also creates a risk that the extent of the threat level can be represented as consistently extreme in the abstract.

Courts have an important role to play in setting the boundaries of what is appropriate action. As was discussed in the previous chapter, the European Court of Human Rights and the Court of Justice of the European Union are highly influential in the creation of surveillance legislation at the domestic level. Their influence stems from their status as the recognised sources of definitive interpretations regarding the implications of Article 8 of the European Convention on Human Rights and Articles 7 and 8 of the Charter of Fundamental Rights of the European Union respectively. The role of supranational courts – free from the pressures of domestic politics – has been central in improving the standards of surveillance governance in Europe. Even though the ECtHR may apply a wide margin of appreciation in the surveillance context, its surveillance decisions have consistently led to increased transparency in domestic surveillance regimes. While the CJEU is a comparative newcomer to the area of privacy adjudication, its rulings have built on the jurisprudence of the ECtHR and have given fresh impetus to the human rights argument for greater controls on surveillance powers.[3]

In Ireland, the courts have recognised an unenumerated right to privacy[4] and have referred several high-profile and influential privacy cases to the CJEU.[5] Chapter 2 of this book discussed how interpretations of the Constitution of the United States by the US Supreme Court have led to changes in executive policies and catalysed legislative reforms in the area of surveillance. As just one example, Title III of the Omnibus Crime Control and Safe Streets Act codified the holding in *Katz v United States* that judicial authorisation must be obtained prior to the conducting of certain forms of domestic surveillance.[6] While the United Kingdom does not have the strong tradition of judicial review that exists in Ireland and the US, it has reformed its surveillance legislation in response to ECtHR and CJEU judgements.[7]

---

3 *Digital Rights Ireland and Seitlinger and Others* [2014] WLR (D) 164; *Tele2 Sverige AB v Post-och telestyrelsen and Secretary of State for the Home Department v Tom Watson and Others* [2017] 2 WLR 1289.

4 *Kennedy v Ireland* [1987] IR 587 (HC).

5 *Digital Rights Ireland and Seitlinger and Others* [2014] WLR (D) 164; *Maximillian Schrems v Data Protection Commissioner* [2016] 2 CMLR 2.

6 *Katz v United States* 389 US 347 (1967).

7 For example, the UK Parliament passed the Interception of Communications Act 1985 in response to the ECtHR decision in *Malone v The United Kingdom* [1984] ECHR 10 and the UK accepted the need to reform its approach to data retention following *Tele2 Sverige AB v Post-och telestyrelsen and Secretary of State for the Home Department v Tom Watson and Others* [2017] 2 WLR 1289.

Moreover, UK domestic courts have played a role in upholding these standards.[8] In addition to this type of high-level review, the judiciary can also play an important role in ensuring accountability of government authorities by excluding evidence from criminal trials. It should be noted, however, that due to the 'intelligence' as opposed to 'prosecutory' focus of much surveillance investigation – not to mention the phenomenon of 'parallel construction'[9] – this judicial power is often less significant in the covert surveillance context.

While high-level constitutional review is very important for the protection of privacy, this chapter begins by focusing on a different type of judicial work that is crucial in the field of surveillance law. As seen in Chapter 2, US courts have traditionally placed significant import on prior judicial authorisation.[10] While the supranational European courts have been less prescriptive on the precise form of review, the courts have placed increasing emphasis on the importance of direct judicial involvement in individual surveillance decisions. While the advantages of judicial review of surveillance decisions were recognised as early as the seminal ECtHR decision in *Klass v Germany*, focus on the safeguard has intensified in recent years.[11] While constitutional decisions are vital for setting the boundaries of protection, in order to understand how powers may be limited in practice, it is necessary to consider the role of the courts on the frontline in surveillance cases. The clearest example of a surveillance judge operating on the frontline is one who is in the position of authorising a surveillance measure. While

8 See *Davis and Others v Secretary of State for the Home Department and Others* [2015] WLR(D) 318 which cited *Digital Rights Ireland and Seitlinger and Others* [2014] WLR (D) 164.

9 For example, US criminal defendants are supposed to be notified if evidence obtained through the Foreign Intelligence Surveillance Court (discussed below) is used in a case against them, yet the Snowden revelations revealed a policy of parallel constructionism to avoid exposing the source of the information. John Shiftman and Kristina Cooke, 'US Directs Agents to Cover Up Program used to Investigate Americans' (*Reuters*, 5 August 2013) <www.reuters.com/article/us-dea-sod-idUSBRE97409R20130805>

10 While the chapter considered some of the challenges to privacy that arise when adjudicating on surveillance matters in criminal cases in ordinary courts, it acknowledged the increased difficulties in the intelligence context.

11 *Roman Zakharov v Russia* [2015] ECHR 1065, 68–69; *Szabo and Vissy v Hungary* [2016] ECHR 579, 73, 75; TJ McIntyre, 'Judicial Oversight of Surveillance: The Case of Ireland in Comparative Perspective' in Martin Scheinin, Helle Krunke, and Marina Aksenova (eds), *Judges as Guardians of Constitutionalism and Human Rights* (Edward Elgar 2016) 19; Maria Helen Murphy, 'Surveillance and the Right to Privacy: Is an "Effective Remedy" Possible?' in Alice Diver and Jacinta Miller (eds), *Justiciability of Human Rights Law in Domestic Jurisdictions* (Springer 2016) 289. See Chapter 3.

it is acknowledged that constitutional courts will face challenges from a political perspective, additional difficulties can arise for the judge interacting more directly with real cases and with limited information. This chapter will also consider the related role of the specialist supervisory judge who oversees the operation of surveillance regimes.

The ECtHR has stated that 'the rule of law implies, *inter alia*, that an interference by the executive authorities with an individual's rights should be subject to an effective control which should normally be assured by the judiciary'.[12] In consideration of the surveillance context, the ECtHR has noted 'in a field where abuse is potentially so easy in individual cases and could have such harmful consequences for democratic society as a whole, it is in principle desirable to entrust supervisory control to a judge'.[13]

In spite of recognising the real risk of abuse of power in the surveillance context, the ECtHR concedes that other supervisory bodies may be permissible so long as they are 'independent of the authorities carrying out the surveillance' and are 'vested with sufficient powers and competence to exercise an effective and continuous control'.[14] Accordingly, the ECtHR has tended to consider 'the totality of the regulatory system' when assessing whether 'adequate and effective guarantees against abuse' exist.[15] This reflects the reality that a supranational court must be cautious about imposing rigid requirements on diverse legal systems – particularly in a field of jealously guarded national interest, like surveillance. The flexible approach of the ECtHR when considering different forms of judicial control also acknowledges the importance of secrecy in the surveillance context where traditional requirements for transparency and openness in court proceedings may be appropriately circumscribed. Indeed, similar issues arise with the obtaining of a surveillance authorisation as arise with the obtaining of a traditional search warrant.

Judicial involvement can occur at any stage of the surveillance process. While the ECtHR has traditionally applied a malleable standard on when the review must take place, the trend appears to be towards requiring prior judicial review for surveillance measures when ECtHR case law – such as *Roman Zakharov v Russia*[16] – is viewed alongside CJEU case law – such

---

12 *Szabo and Vissy v Hungary* [2016] ECHR 579, 77.

13 *Klass and Others v Germany* (1979) 2 EHRR 214, 56.

14 *Klass and Others v Germany* (1979) 2 EHRR 214, 56.

15 TJ McIntyre, 'Judicial Oversight of Surveillance: The Case of Ireland in Comparative Perspective' in Martin Scheinin, Helle Krunke, and Marina Aksenova (eds), *Judges as Guardians of Constitutionalism and Human Rights* (Edward Elgar 2016).

16 *Roman Zakharov v Russia* [2015] ECHR 1065, 258. See also *Szabo and Vissy v Hungary* [2016] ECHR 579, 77; and *Telegraaf Media v the Netherlands* [2012] ECHR 1965, 100–102.

as *Digital Rights Ireland*[17] and *Tele2 and Watson*.[18] Requiring review prior to the conducting of surveillance measures – in addition to providing for subsequent review – is certainly desirable from the perspectives of transparency and accountability. What is important to highlight, however, is that courts (and quasi-judicial bodies) tend to operate differently in the surveillance context. In spite of this, it is essential to consider whether the checks provided can adequately limit the exercise of surveillance power. Judges and quasi-judicial bodies should not be inserted into the surveillance process as a form of 'judicial washing' where the legitimacy of the judicial tradition is exploited in order to avoid real scrutiny of surveillance practices.

The judicial and quasi-judicial bodies that this chapter focuses on are specialised surveillance courts and bodies. In general, specialised courts are created for numerous reasons. One reason is that specialist bodies can bring a level of substantive and procedural expertise to issues that is particularly important in technical areas.[19] This is one of the arguments in favour of having reviews of surveillance requests carried out by judges with significant experience and familiarity with surveillance cases. In addition to ensuring a more specialist knowledge and understanding of the technical issues in surveillance cases, such specialisation can also avoid the bamboozling of judges who are accustomed to a more general docket with the executive attested risks of not granting a surveillance request. If a judge consistently deals with a similar type of case, there is an argument that they will be better positioned to conduct comparative scrutiny and to identify cases that raise questions of proportionality and necessity. The disadvantages of specialisation include problems of bias. Where a court or group of judges become overly familiar with an agency that frequently appears before it – generally ex parte – there is a significant risk of capture. An alternative perspective may be that a court with growing expertise may be overly inclined to 'substitute their judgment for an agency . . . creating an overly dominant oversight body'.[20]

---

17 In *Digital Rights Ireland*, the CJEU criticised that 'access by the competent national authorities to the data retained is not made dependent on a prior review carried out by a court or by an independent administrative body whose decision seeks to limit access to the data and their use to what is strictly necessary for the purpose of attaining the objective pursued and which intervenes following a reasoned request of those authorities submitted within the framework of procedures of prevention, detection or criminal prosecutions'. *Digital Rights Ireland and Seitlinger and Others* [2014] WLR (D) 164, 62.

18 *Tele2 Sverige AB v Post-och telestyrelsen and Secretary of State for the Home Department v Tom Watson and Others* [2017] 2 WLR 1289.

19 Harold Bruff, 'Specialized Courts in Administrative Law' (1991) 43 *Administrative Law Review* 329.

20 Harold Bruff, 'Specialized Courts in Administrative Law' (1991) 43 *Administrative Law Review* 329.

Ireland: the 'Designated Judge' and the 'Complaints Referee'

Many governments have been hesitant to provide for traditional judicial involvement in surveillance cases. Irish surveillance law provides a useful case study that demonstrates such reticence. The Irish surveillance regime is comprised of a number of different statutes governing particular types of surveillance. The Criminal Justice (Surveillance) Act 2009, for example, governs the use of 'surveillance devices' and provides for prior judicial authorisation in the form of a District Court judge.[21] Reflecting how procedures must be designed to account for the importance of secrecy in this area, the authorisation process takes place *in camera* and otherwise than in public. While the Communications (Retention of Data) Act 2011 – enacted to implement the now invalid Data Retention Directive – does not provide for judicial involvement at the point where the government authority makes a request for retained data,[22] the Irish government has expressed an intention to change this process in the wake of *Digital Rights Ireland* and *Tele2 Sverige*.[23] The Interception of Postal Packets and Telecommunications Messages (Regulation) Act 1993 also does not provide for judicial involvement at the authorisation stage. The lack of prior judicial authorisation would appear to raise questions under current understandings of the human rights requirements, but quasi-judicial safeguards that each regime does have in common, however, are supervision by a person appointed as the 'Designated Judge' and a procedure for individual redress provided by the appointment of a 'Complaints Referee'.

A Designated Judge is a serving High Court judge appointed to oversee each of the surveillance regimes and to assess whether the relevant law is being complied with.[24] The Designated Judge is empowered to investigate

---

21 The Criminal Justice (Surveillance) Act, s 4(1)(2)(3). In cases of urgency, surveillance will sometimes be possible without judicial authorisation for a period of up to 72 hours. The Criminal Justice (Surveillance) Act, s 5.

22 The Communications (Retention of Data) Act 2011, s 6.

23 *Digital Rights Ireland and Seitlinger and Others* [2014] WLR (D) 164; *Tele2 Sverige AB v Post-och telestyrelsen and Secretary of State for the Home Department v Tom Watson and Others* [2017] 2 WLR 1289. General Scheme of the Communications (Retention of Data) Bill 2017; see also John Murray, 'Review of the Law on the Retention of and Access to Communications Data' (April 2017) <www.justice.ie/en/JELR/Review_of_the_Law_on_Retention_of_and_Access_to_Communications_Data.pdf/Files/Review_of_the_Law_on_Retention_of_and_Access_to_Communications_Data.pdf>

24 The Interception of Postal Packets and Telecommunications Messages (Regulation) Act 1993, s 8; The Communications (Retention of Data) Act 2011, ss 11–12. The appointed

the operation of the relevant surveillance regime and is tasked with providing an annual report to the Taoiseach, who must cause a copy of the report to be laid before the Oireachtas. The Designated Judge is given significant discretion in their role and is entitled to access and inspect any official documents relating to a relevant surveillance measure. As pointed out by Murphy and Kennedy '[t]he freedom granted to the Designated Judge to decide what is appropriate to place in the annual report has resulted in very little substantive information being made available to the public'.[25] Unfortunately, the reports released by the Designated Judge – particularly under the Interception Act and Retention of Data Act[26] – have tended to be terse and unilluminating. The fact that the inspections of each relevant investigatory organisation with surveillance powers appear to take place over the space of a day does little to reassure regarding the breadth or depth of the review being carried out.[27] The limited nature of the review could be said to be 'designed-in' by the fact that the Designated Judge must carry out their duties in addition to their role as a High Court judge without any additional resources or technical expertise being made available.[28]

If an individual believes that they have been the subject of a surveillance measure under one of the Acts, they may make a complaint to the Complaints Referee.[29] This body was initially established as a system of redress under the Interception Act but its jurisdiction has been expanded to the

Designated Judge under the Interception Act also serves as the Designated Judge for the Retention of Data Act. A different Designated Judge is appointed to review the operation of the Surveillance Act. The Criminal Justice (Surveillance) Act, s 12.

25 Rónán Kennedy and Maria Helen Murphy, *Information and Communications Technology Law in Ireland* (Clarus 2017) 150.

26 In spite of no significant difference between the requirements laid out for the report of the Designated Judge under the Surveillance Act, the form and content of the Surveillance Act reports have tended to be more detailed than the reports that have typically been provided under the Interception Act and Retention of Data Act. While the greater detail of the reports provides additional transparency in comparative terms, the reports remain vague and provide minimal oversight into the extent of the activities conducted and the manner in which they are carried out.

27 See for example Digital Rights Ireland, 'Surveillance Library' <www.digitalrights.ie/ irish-surveillancedocuments/>

28 Maria Helen Murphy, 'Surveillance and the Right to Privacy: Is an "Effective Remedy" Possible?' in Alice Diver and Jacinta Miller (eds), *Justiciability of Human Rights Law in Domestic Jurisdictions* (Springer 2016) 289, 302; Alisdair Gillespie, 'Covert Surveillance, Human Rights and the Law' (2009) 19(3) *Irish Criminal Law Journal* 71, 75.

29 Interception of Postal Packets and Telecommunications Messages (Regulation) Act 1993, s 9; The Criminal Justice (Surveillance) Act 2009, s 11; The Communications (Retention of Data) Act 2011, s 10.

Surveillance Act and the Retention of Data Act subsequently. When the Interception Act was drafted, it was thought that due to the inherently secretive nature of interceptions it was 'necessary to restrict access to the ordinary courts and instead establish alternative forums of accountability'.[30] The Complaints Referee may be a Circuit or District Court judge or a practising barrister or solicitor of not fewer than 10 years' standing. Thus far, however, the Complaints Referees appointed have been judges. If a complaint is neither 'frivolous nor vexatious', the Complaints Referee will investigate. If a contravention of the relevant Act is found, the Complaints Referee has the power to quash the surveillance authorisation and recommend the payment of compensation. While the open jurisdiction provides theoretically broad access to the complaints mechanism, the absence of a notification mechanism under any of the Acts undermines its significance in practice. There is remarkably little insight into the operation of the system. There is no official reporting of decisions or statistics, and there is no evidence of any successful complaints under the Complaints Referee mechanism since its introduction.[31]

In spite of the surface level involvement of independent oversight in the Irish surveillance laws, the practical effect of these safeguards has been less than satisfactory.[32] The ineffectiveness of the Irish system of quasi-judicial oversight demonstrates how the role of such bodies must be carefully set out in law and how appropriate resources must be provided if such bodies are to carry out their duties adequately.

The United Kingdom: the Investigatory Powers Commissioner and Judicial Commissioners

This history of judicial involvement in UK surveillance operations is interesting. The UK had its system of oversight approved in *Kennedy v The United Kingdom* in spite of its entirely internal authorisation process. In reaching its judgment, the ECtHR placed significant emphasis on the

---

30 Dáil Éireann Debate (19 May 1993) 431(1) <www.oireachtas.ie/en/debates/debate/dail/1993-05-13/>; Rónán Kennedy and Maria Helen Murphy, *Information and Communications Technology Law in Ireland* (Clarus 2017) 149.

31 TJ McIntyre, 'Judicial Oversight of Surveillance: The Case of Ireland in Comparative Perspective' in Martin Scheinin, Helle Krunke, and Marina Aksenova (eds), *Judges as Guardians of Constitutionalism and Human Rights* (Edward Elgar 2016).

32 TJ McIntyre, 'Judicial Oversight of Surveillance: The Case of Ireland in Comparative Perspective' in Martin Scheinin, Helle Krunke, and Marina Aksenova (eds), *Judges as Guardians of Constitutionalism and Human Rights* (Edward Elgar 2016).

Investigatory Powers Tribunal and the Interception of Communications Commissioner[33] which together provided a degree of ex post review and oversight of the RIPA internal interception regime.[34] The ECtHR praised the 'independent and impartial' nature of the IPT and spoke approvingly of the fact that the members of the IPT were required to hold or have held high judicial office or to be experienced lawyers.[35] The ECtHR highlighted that the Interception of Communications Commissioner – tasked at the time with overseeing the general functioning of the UK interception regime and producing reports – was independent of the executive and the legislature.[36]

Subsequent to the Snowden revelations, the UK surveillance regime was brought under fresh scrutiny – particularly in light of the level and form of surveillance occurring that did not appear to have an adequate legal basis. This led to the drafting of the Investigatory Powers Act which provides a 'comprehensive legislative framework for the conduct of technological surveillance' for a vast array of surveillance powers.[37] The tactic adopted to mitigate concerns regarding the privacy implications of the Act was to promise a 'world-leading oversight regime' designed to ensure that the powers were exercised appropriately.[38] Prior to the publication of the IPA, the Royal United Services Institute for Defence and Security Studies (RUSIDSS) produced a report that highlighted the importance of holding investigatory bodies to account. In light of its conclusion that it is 'neither possible nor desirable' to render appropriately secret operations 'fully

---

33 Under the Regulation of Investigatory Powers Act 2000, a number of different oversight bodies were appointed to oversee and report on the different surveillance activities. The IPA abolished the offices of the Interception of Communications Commissioner, the Intelligence Services Commissioner, the Chief Surveillance Commissioner and the Scottish Chief Surveillance Commissioner, and the ordinary Surveillance Commissioners and Scottish Surveillance Commissioners. The Regulation of Investigatory Powers Act 2000 s 240(1) (a) – (f); Simon McKay, *Blackstone's Guide to the Investigatory Powers Act 2016* (Oxford University Press 2017) 208.

34 *Kennedy v The United Kingdom* [2010] ECHR 682.

35 *Kennedy v The United Kingdom* [2010] ECHR 682, 167. Moreover, the ECtHR also approved of the fact that the IPT had a number of powers, including the power to access closed material, to quash orders, to require the destruction of surveillance material, and to order that compensation be paid.

36 *Kennedy v The United Kingdom* [2010] ECHR 682, 166.

37 Simon McKay, *Blackstone's Guide to the Investigatory Powers Act 2016* (Oxford University Press 2017) 2.

38 Theresa May, 'Home Secretary: Publication of the Draft Investigatory Powers Bill' (4 November 2015) <www.gov.uk/government/speeches/home-secretary-publication-of-draft-investigatory-powers-bill>

transparent', RUSIDSS maintains that 'effective oversight is therefore all the more essential'. RUSIDSS criticised the existing system for having developed in an ad hoc manner and with limited public knowledge. Accordingly, RUSIDSS argued that '[r]eorganisation and better resourcing of the existing setup could create a more streamlined, robust and systematic oversight regime that would be genuinely visible to the public and have a positive effect' on the investigatory authorities.[39]

While the IPT was retained with some reforms,[40] the numerous specialist surveillance commissioners were abolished and replaced with the Investigatory Powers Commissioner and Judicial Commissioners.[41] A highly touted element of this 'world-leading oversight regime' was to be the introduction of a new ex ante system of surveillance authorisation. There are some differences in the various sections of the IPA, so the process of obtaining a targeted interception warrant will be considered as an illustration. The intercepting authority must first approach the Secretary of State – ie a member of the executive branch – who must consider whether the warrant is necessary, proportionate, and whether satisfactory arrangements have been made.[42] Second, the decision to issue the warrant must be approved by a Judicial Commissioner.[43]

The then Minister of State, Minister for Security, John Hayes, posited that 'through the change to authorisation, we have, for the first time, and in highly significant – one might even say groundbreaking – terms, struck an important balance between the role of the Executive and the role of the judiciary'.[44] This system of interception approval was described as a 'double-lock' by the government. The use of the term 'double-lock' is quite misleading as it appears to imply that the involvement of both a Judicial Commissioner and a Secretary of State leads to a particularly robust level

---

39 Royal United Services Institute for Defence and Security Studies, Report of the Independent Surveillance Review, A Democratic Licence to Operate (July 2015) <https://rusi.org/sites/default/files/20150714_whr_2-15_a_democratic_licence_to_operate.pdf>

40 In addition to having its jurisdiction expanded, there is now a right of appeal against a decision of the Investigatory Powers Tribunal in certain circumstance. Simon McKay, *Blackstone's Guide to the Investigatory Powers Act 2016* (Oxford University Press 2017) 207, 218.

41 IPA, s 240(1)(a)–(f). Simon McKay, *Blackstone's Guide to the Investigatory Powers Act 2016* (Oxford University Press 2017) 209.

42 Including for example safeguards relating to the disclosing of the data. IPA, s 19(1)(a)–(c) and (3)(a)–(c). Simon McKay, *Blackstone's Guide to the Investigatory Powers Act 2016* (Oxford University Press 2017) 51.

43 IPA, s 19(1)(d) and (3)(d). Unless the warrant is viewed as urgent in which case a different procedure applies. Simon McKay, *Blackstone's Guide to the Investigatory Powers Act 2016* (Oxford University Press 2017) 51.

44 HC Deb, 6 June 2016, vol 611, col 878.

of review. Importantly, the Judicial Commissioner does not carry out a full factual inquiry but considers the decision of the Secretary of State on the grounds of proportionality and necessity under the standards of 'judicial review'.[45] This review must be carried out with a 'sufficient degree of care' so as to ensure compliance with the general duties in relation to privacy.[46] Karemba questions the inclusion of the standard of judicial review due its 'multifarious meanings' and points out how critics of the IPA have rejected the government's choice of terminology of a 'double-lock'.[47] While the involvement of the Judicial Commissioner at the preauthorisation stage would appear to lend a degree of independence and legitimacy to the system, McKay points out it is 'judicial approval' and not 'judicial authorisation'.[48] If the procedure is to be considered authentic judicial authorisation, standards need to be clearly set out to ensure that Judicial Commissioners conduct full assessments independent of the decisions of the Secretary of State.[49]

The IPC also carries out ex post facto oversight under the IPA.[50] It has been argued that this dual role could be construed as having the Judicial Commissioners 'mark their own homework' in a way that could 'dilute the credibility and independence of the new body',[51] but a number of important safeguards are worth discussing. A crucial form of ex post facto

45 IPA, s 20.
46 As imposed by IPA, s 20. There is an opportunity to appeal the decision of a Judicial Commissioner to the Investigatory Powers Commissioner if an approval is not granted. IPA, s 23.
47 Byron Karemba, 'The Investigatory Powers Bill: Introducing Judicial Authorisation of Surveillance Warrants in the United Kingdom – Putting the "Double-Lock" in Focus (Part I)' (UK Constitutional Law Blog, 22 March 2016) <https://ukconstitutionallaw.org/>
48 Simon McKay, *Blackstone's Guide to the Investigatory Powers Act 2016* (Oxford University Press 2017) 55.
49 While the Office of the Investigatory Powers Tribunal has stated that Judicial Commissioners will be applying a higher standard of review than Wednesbury, it also notes that the Secretary of State is the primary decision maker under the Act with the Judicial Commissioner acting as an independent safeguard. Investigatory Powers Commissioner's Office, Advisory Notice 1/2018 Approval of Warrants, Authorisations and Notices by Judicial Commissioners (8 March 2018) 5 <https://ipco.org.uk/docs/20180403%20IPCO%20Guidance%20Note%202.pdf>
50 IPA, s 229. It should be noted that the Secretary of State is empowered to modify the functions of the IPC as regards their ex post facto oversight functions. IPA, s 239. Although such modifications should not alter any power to 'approve, quash or cancel' an authorisation or warrant, or the variation or renewal of an authorisation or warrant. Byron Karemba, 'The Investigatory Powers Bill: Putting the Investigatory Powers Commissioner in Focus (Part II)' (UK Constitutional Law Blog, 15 April 2016) <https://ukconstitutionallaw.org/>
51 Joint Committee on the Draft Investigatory Powers Bill Written evidence to the Joint Committee on the Draft Investigatory Powers Bill 675–687, 683 <http://data.parliament.uk/

oversight and transparency is provided in the form of yearly reports regarding the operation of the Judicial Commissioners.[52] While the first report of the IPC is yet to be released, the IPA will require reports to include statistics on the use of surveillance powers, information regarding the results and impact of such use, the operation of the safeguards provided by the IPA, and information about the work of the Technology Advisory Panel, among other information.[53] Another form of transparency is provided by the duty of the IPC to inform a person of any 'serious' error relating to them if it is in the public interest for the person to be informed.[54] While this is an important protection, it is limited by the fact that the IPC may not decide that an error is serious unless the error has caused significant prejudice or harm to the person concerned. Crucially, 'the fact that there has been a breach of a person's Convention rights (within the meaning of the Human Rights Act 1998) is not sufficient by itself for an error to be a serious error'.[55]

In spite of its shortcomings, the oversight provided by the IPC is certainly superior to that provided by the Designated Judge and Complaints Referee systems in Ireland. There is far greater transparency provided by the UK system. For example, the detailed requirements regarding the reporting obligation – while not beyond reproach – put the superficiality of the equivalent safeguard in the Irish system into sharp relief. While the system of error reporting is limited, it does provide for some degree of post-surveillance notification that is another important safeguard in the secretive surveillance context.[56] Even though it would be expected that a jurisdiction of the size (and with the surveillance capabilities) of the UK would allocate significantly more funding to an oversight body than Ireland, the difference in approach to establishing appropriate resources, support, and expertise for the oversight body is striking. The Investigatory Powers Commissioner's Office is planned to comprise not only the current IPC (Lord Justice Sir Adrian Fulford) but around 70 staff including a Technical Advisory Panel

---

writtenevidence/committeeevidence.svc/evidencedocument/draft-investigatory-powers-bill-committee/draft-investigatory-powers-bill/written/26352.html>

52 IPA, s 234. The Prime Minister must publish an annual report subject to redactions.

53 IPA, s 234.

54 IPA, s 231.

55 IPA, s 231(3).

56 The European Court of Human Rights has held that the notification of interception of communications is 'inextricably linked to the effectiveness of remedies before the courts' *Roman Zakharov v Russia* [2015] ECHR 1065, 286; *Klass and Others v Germany* (1979) 2 EHRR 214, 57, and *Weber and Saravia v Germany* [2006] ECHR 1173, 135.

of scientific experts, lawyers, and communications experts.[57] In spite of this, the manner in which the IPC and Judicial Commissioners are funded and appointed raises questions regarding institutional independence. The IPA states that the Secretary of State has the authority – albeit in consultation with the IPC[58] – to provide the Judicial Commissioners with 'such staff, and such accommodation, equipment and other facilities and services as the Secretary of State considers necessary for the carrying out Commissioners' functions'.[59] As pointed out by Lord Judge '[t]he idea that judges will be looking at the Home Secretary's decisions and saying, "We do not think that is right", and then going cap in hand to that same Minister is not a sufficient separation'.[60] Furthermore, it is the Prime Minister who has authority to appoint the IPC and the other Judicial Commissioners.[61]

The United States: the Foreign Intelligence Surveillance Court

In the 1970s, the US Senate's Church Committee identified a number of institutional flaws that enabled the abuse of power by US intelligence agencies. The flaws included the 'ambiguous laws and fuzzy instructions' that governed the operation of the intelligence agencies,[62] the assumption of 'absolute and permanent secrecy',[63] and a lack of oversight.[64] In addition to the formation of specially designed oversight committees in Congress,

57 Investigatory Powers Commissioner's Office, 'Who We Are' (IPCO, 27 August 2017) <www.ipco.org.uk>
58 And subject to the approval of the Treasury.
59 IPA, ss 238(1)(2)(3).
60 Joint Committee on the Draft Investigatory Powers Bill Oral evidence: Draft Investigatory Powers Bill, HC 651, Wednesday 2 December 2015, Q 56–57. Byron Karemba, 'The Investigatory Powers Bill: Putting the Investigatory Powers Commissioner in Focus (Part II)' (UK Constitutional Law Blog, 15 April 2016).
61 IPA, ss 227–228.
62 Including the use of flexible terms that could be interpreted broadly such as 'subversion' and 'national security'. Frederick Schwarz and Aziz Huq, *Unchecked and Unbalanced Presidential Power in a Time of Terror* (The New Press 2008) 5; Walter Mondale, Robert Stein, and Caitlinrose Fisher, 'No Longer a Neutral Magistrate: The Foreign Intelligence Surveillance Court in the Wake of the War on Terror' (2016) 100 *Minnesota Law Review* 2261.
63 See Church Committee Report, Book I, 11–12. Walter Mondale, Robert Stein, and Caitlinrose Fisher, 'No Longer a Neutral Magistrate: The Foreign Intelligence Surveillance Court in the Wake of the War on Terror' (2016) 100 *Minnesota Law Review* 2261.
64 Church Committee Report, Book I, 11. Walter Mondale, Robert Stein, and Caitlinrose Fisher, 'No Longer a Neutral Magistrate: The Foreign Intelligence Surveillance Court in the Wake of the War on Terror' (2016) 100 *Minnesota Law Review* 2261.

the Church Committee also led to the enactment of the Foreign Intelligence Surveillance Act 1978 (FISA).[65] FISA set out a legal framework for intelligence agencies and also created the Foreign Intelligence Surveillance Court (FISC) as a specialised court established to review and approve government applications to carry out surveillance measures. While the FISC was formed in response to the Church Committee revelations that exposed the overreach of intelligence agencies over several decades and government administrations,[66] the Snowden revelations confirmed how far the FISC had 'veered off course from their original design'.[67] While the FISC was initially conceived as a court tasked to consider and grant legitimate surveillance applications, the Snowden revelations confirmed that it had transformed into a 'regulatory body that issued long opinions secretly approving surveillance programs that Congress had never considered – and likely would not have approved'.[68] There is some logic to the holding of surveillance court proceedings ex parte and otherwise than in public when the proceedings are comparable to traditional search warrant proceedings. Where the proceedings are dealing with broader matters – such as the bulk adjudication of programmatic surveillance – the arguments for closed door and ex parte proceedings dissipate.

While legislative action facilitated the shift of the FISC away from its original role, the implications of the changes could not have been foreseen based on a plain reading of the relevant legislation.[69] While the government

---

65 Foreign Intelligence Surveillance Act 1978, s 103(a).

66 US Government and Senate, Report of the Select Committee to Study Governmental Operations with Respect to Intelligence Activities (14 April 1976) No 94-755, viii <www.intelligence.senate.gov/sites/default/files/94755_II.pdf>

67 Walter Mondale, Robert Stein, and Caitlinrose Fisher, 'No Longer a Neutral Magistrate: The Foreign Intelligence Surveillance Court in the Wake of the War on Terror' (2016) 100 *Minnesota Law Review* 2251, 2254.

68 Orin Kerr, 'A Rule of Lenity for National Security Surveillance Law' (2014) 100(7) *Virginia Law Review* 1513, 1514.

69 Uniting and Strengthening America by Providing Appropriate Tools Required to Intercept and Obstruct Terrorism (USA PATRIOT) Act of 2001, Public Law No 107-56; Foreign Intelligence Surveillance Act of 1978 Amendments Act of 2008, Public Law No 110-261. For example, in a USA PATRIOT Act amendment to FISA in 2001, the language of section 1804(a)(7)(B) that previously required that 'the purpose' of the surveillance was to obtain foreign intelligence information, was changed to require only that 'a significant purpose' was to obtain foreign intelligence information. This change in language 'essentially dismantled the "wall" between law enforcement officials and intelligence officials, which was "designed to protect against using the secretive foreign intelligence collection process in order to build a criminal case"'. Michael Francel, 'Rubber-Stamping: Legislative, Executive, and Judicial Responses to Critiques of the Foreign Intelligence Surveillance Court One Year after the 2013 NSA Leaks' (2014) 66(2) *Administrative Law Review* 409, 420–421.

had previously relied on the President's 'inherent constitutional authority' to engage in the bulk collection of communications metadata, the executive branch sought to legitimise the surveillance programmes through the FISC. In a notable example revealed by the Snowden documents, the FISC ruled that the telephone records of all Americans could be considered 'relevant' to authorised international terrorism investigations under section 215 of the USA PATRIOT Act as they could be used in a future search.[70]

The FISC pointed out that 'information concerning known and unknown affiliates of international terrorist organizations was contained within the non-content metadata the government sought to obtain'.[71] In a distortion of the standard, the FISC effectively concluded that 'because collecting irrelevant data was necessary to identify relevant data, the irrelevant data could thereby be deemed relevant'.[72] While the FISC did place some limitations on the circumstances under which the collected phone records could be looked at, this assessment was to be made by the NSA and not by the FISC. This confirmed the system of programmatic collection and placed FISC in the role of 'approving standards for searches but not the searches themselves'.[73] Delivering a broad ruling of this nature is very different from granting a warrant in an individual case. In fact, it resembles an Act of rule-making. This is clearly problematic from a rule of law perspective where the substance of the ruling is intended to remain secret.

In 2015, Congress passed the USA FREEDOM Act in response to the Snowden revelations.[74] The law was designed to reform the bulk collection of records under Section 215 of the USA PATRIOT Act and made efforts to

---

70 *In Re Application of the Federal Bureau of Investigation for an Order Requiring the Production of Tangible Things from [Redacted]* No BR 13-109, slip op, 28-29 (FISA Ct 2013) <www.fisc.uscourts.gov/sites/default/files/ BR%2013-109%20Order-1.pdf>. Walter Mondale, Robert Stein, and Caitlinrose Fisher, 'No Longer a Neutral Magistrate: The Foreign Intelligence Surveillance Court in the Wake of the War on Terror' (2016) 100 *Minnesota Law Review* 2265. Following the Snowden revelations, the Second Circuit held that 'relevant' had been interpreted too broadly. *American Civil Liberties Union v Clapper,* 785 F3d 787 (2d Cir 2015). See also the subsequent *In Re Application of the Federal Bureau of Investigation for an Order Requiring the Production of Tangible Things* No BR 15-75, slip op, 10 (FISA Ct, 29 June 2015).

71 *In Re Application of the Federal Bureau of Investigation for an Order Requiring the Production of Tangible Things from [Redacted]* No BR 13-109, 20 (FISA Ct, 29 August 2013) <www.uscourts.gov/uscourts/courts/fisc/br13-09-primary-order.pdf>

72 Elizabeth Goitein and Faiza Patel, 'What went wrong with the FISA Court' (Brennan Center for Justice at New York University School of Law, 18 March 2015) 22 <www.brennancenter.org/sites/default/files/analysis/What_Went_%20Wrong_With_The_FISA_Court.pdf>

73 Elizabeth Goitein and Faiza Patel, 'What went wrong with the FISA Court' (Brennan Center for Justice at New York University School of Law, 18 March 2015) 22 <www.brennancenter.org/sites/default/files/analysis/What_Went_%20Wrong_With_The_FISA_Court.pdf>

74 The USA Freedom Act, Public Law No 114-23.

address the undermining of the role of the FISC as an effective authorisation body. Two key ways the Act set out to achieve this goal was to include a requirement to publish opinions in certain circumstances and to allow for the appointment of amicus curiae.[75] The provision made for the declassification of FISC opinions that include 'a significant construction or interpretation of any provision of law'[76] 'to the greatest extent practicable' marks some progress against the prevalence of secret interpretations of law in this area.[77] Risks remain, of course, that the term 'significant' could be interpreted overly narrowly. This is suboptimal from a transparency perspective as '[w]hat is insignificant in the eyes of the Attorney General may be significant to the American citizen whose information may be impermissibly obtained under that interpretation'.[78] If effective control is to be exercised – and opportunities for abuse are to be minimised – it would seem clear that publication should be the norm and not the exception. Unsurprisingly, a 'national security' waiver can prevent declassification, which is a standard also at clear risk of manipulation. The Act does provide, however, that a summary of the relevant interpretation must be published.[79] The FREEDOM Act also provides for a limited special advocacy system where amici may be appointed to argue where in the opinion of the court, an application 'presents a novel or significant interpretation of the law'.[80] While special advocates have the potential to provide an important safeguard against judicial capture, ambiguities in the statutory language have the potential to undermine their effectiveness.

Mondale, Stein, and Fisher argue that the structural problems that enabled the previous expansion of power were not addressed by the FREEDOM Act and maintain that 'Congress replaced one broad and ambiguous statutory directive with another'. Kerr calls for an interesting alternative approach by endorsing the enactment of an interpretive 'rule of lenity' by the US Congress.[81] Under Kerr's formulation:

> When the government's power under existing law is ambiguous, the FISC should adopt the narrowed construction that favors the

---

75 See The USA Freedom Act, ss 401–402. Walter Mondale, Robert Stein, and Caitlinrose Fisher, 'No Longer a Neutral Magistrate: The Foreign Intelligence Surveillance Court in the Wake of the War on Terror' (2016) 100 *Minnesota Law Review* 2269.

76 Including a 'specific selection term'.

77 The USA Freedom Act, Public Law No 114-23, ss 402 and 602.

78 Walter Mondale, Robert Stein, and Caitlinrose Fisher, 'No Longer a Neutral Magistrate: The Foreign Intelligence Surveillance Court in the Wake of the War on Terror' (2016) 100 *Minnesota Law Review* 2291.

79 The USA Freedom Act, Public Law No 114-23, s 602(c).

80 The USA Freedom Act, Public Law No 114-23, s 279.

81 Orin Kerr, 'A Rule of Lenity for National Security Surveillance Law' (2014) 100(7) *Virginia Law Review* 1513, 1514.

individual instead of the State. If the executive wants new surveillance powers, it should go to Congress for those powers instead of to the courts. Within constitutional boundaries, the power to define national security law will rest with the elected branches, and in turn, with the people.

By circumscribing the role of the judiciary in this manner, Kerr places the decision-making power in the hands of the legislature. Part of Kerr's reasoning rests on the logic that the legislature will be held to account by virtue of a 'feedback loop that allows the public to control the scope of government powers through the elected branches'.[82] Kerr additionally contends that Congress are better placed than the judiciary to 'draw the appropriate lines of power'.[83] Kerr acknowledges that a rule of lenity would not be a panacea as there is no guarantee that the courts would follow it, however, such a rule would be a useful first step to encourage more transparent surveillance laws.

There is much to recommend a general rule of lenity in the interpretation of surveillance legislation and it could potentially lead to more clarity in the drafting of surveillance legislation. In some ways, similar ideas are represented in the ECtHR's rules regarding legality and foreseeability. On the other hand, outside of the US context, the institutional structures of government may not always be compatible with Kerr's reasoning regarding the role of the legislative branch. Compare, for example, the branches of the US Government with the Irish and UK systems. Even though the Irish and UK systems provide for a technical distinction between the executive and legislative branches, the appointment of the Taoiseach and Prime Minister – and the formation of the Cabinet – from the ranks of the party or coalition in power blurs the boundaries significantly. The success of such a solution is also somewhat contingent on politicians actually wanting to restrict the scope of surveillance measures. While many politicians may make gestures towards the protection of privacy and other civil liberties, a number of recent examples – including the Public Services Card discussed in Chapter 5 – suggest that such talk is just that.

---

82 Orin Kerr, 'A Rule of Lenity for National Security Surveillance Law' (2014) 100(7) *Virginia Law Review* 1513, 1514.
83 Orin Kerr, 'A Rule of Lenity for National Security Surveillance Law' (2014) 100(7) *Virginia Law Review* 1513, 1514.

Open justice in the covert context

The judiciary undoubtedly has a vital role to play in the limitation of surveillance powers. It is also clear that judicial involvement in the granting of surveillance warrants and in the carrying out of surveillance reviews can potential become 'an exercise in rubber-stamping'.[84] It is crucial that all branches of government are involved in the oversight of surveillance activities.[85] The quasi-judicial nature of the oversight systems in the UK and Ireland mean that the oversight authorities rely on the support of the legislature and executive to carry out their roles effectively – particularly in relation to resources and independence. This dynamic heightens the importance of transparency.

Rudenstein points out that the FISC has undermined its own legitimacy and it is unlikely that the court can redeem itself and regain the public's trust 'in the absence of meaningful reform legislation and sufficient disclosures by the FISC that establish that it is in fact insisting upon meaningful judicial accountability'.[86] The discussion of the FISC in this chapter demonstrates how a specialised court can be co-opted by the executive branch. In addition to a lack of technical expertise, the FISC also suffers from a dearth of information 'regarding the ways in which the government is actually implementing its surveillance authority'.[87] It is now known that the FISC made repeated attempts to place limits on intelligence activities, but were faced with frequent and recurring non-compliance by the government agencies.[88] The persistent attempts of the FISC to compel the executive branch to comply with its orders illustrate that while the Court was not necessarily complicit in the executive overreach, it had very little power to reign

---

84 UNHCR, Twenty-seventh Session June 2014 'Report of the UN High Commissioner for Human Rights on The Right to Privacy in a Digital Age' (30 June 2014) A/HRC/27/37 12–13.

85 UNHCR, Twenty-seventh-session June 2014 'Report of the UN High Commissioner for Human Rights on The Right to Privacy in a Digital Age' (30 June 2014) A/HRC/27/37 12–13; TJ McIntyre, 'Judicial Oversight of Surveillance: The Case of Ireland in Comparative Perspective' in Martin Scheinin, Helle Krunke, and Marina Aksenova (eds), *Judges as Guardians of Constitutionalism and Human Rights* (Edward Elgar 2016).

86 David Rudenstine, *The Age of Deference: The Supreme Court, National Security and the Constitutional Order* (Oxford University Press 2016) 149–150.

87 Emily Berman, 'The Two Faces of the Foreign Intelligence Surveillance Court' (2016) 91 *Indiana Law Journal* 1191, 1206.

88 Opinion and Order, *In Re [REDACTED]* No PR/TT (FISA Ct, 14 July 2004) 83–84; *In Re Production of Tangible Things from [REDACTED]* No BR 08-13 (FISA Ct, 28 January 2009).

in executive actions.[89] A FISC judge[90] has commented that the FISC 'does not have the capacity to investigate issues of noncompliance, and in that respect the FISC is in the same position as any other court when it comes to enforcing [government] compliance with its orders'.[91] While it is true that the judiciary must 'ultimately depend upon the aid of the executive arm even for the efficacy of its judgments',[92] courts benefit when decisions are made public as the executive cannot ignore such orders with the degree of impunity they may enjoy when hidden from public view.

The clear takeaway is that if oversight bodies are to operate as an adequate check on executive power, such oversight must be designed carefully, with provision made for appropriate resources, expertise, and independence. Most importantly, transparency must be built in as the default and central value. Designing oversight mechanisms in this way will be the best guarantee against the institutions becoming a fig leaf for surveillance, and providing '"oversight" in name only'.[93]

89 Michael Francel, 'Rubber-Stamping: Legislative, Executive, and Judicial Responses to Critiques of the Foreign Intelligence Surveillance Court One Year after the 2013 NSA Leaks' (2014) 66(2) *Administrative Law Review* 409, 429.
90 Judge Reggie Walton.
91 Carol Leonnig, 'Court: Abilio to Police US Spying Program Limited' *The Washington Post* (Washington, 15 August 2013 <www.washingtonpost.com/politics/court-ability-to-police-us-spyingprogram-limited/2013/08/15/4a8c8c44-05cd-11e3-a07f-49ddc7417125_story.html> (alteration in original) (quoting Judge Reggie Walton).
92 *The Federalist* No 78, 394 (Alexander Hamilton).
93 Glenn Greenwald, 'FISA Court Oversight: A Look Inside a Secret and Empty Process', *The Guardian* (London, 18 June 2013) <www.theguardian.com/commentisfree/2013/jun/19/fisa-court-oversight-process-secrecy>

5　Intentional ambiguity

The role of the legislature

Law is the 'vehicle by which democracy operates; it is the expression of democratic ideals or choices'.[1] The modern democratic vision recognises the legislative branch as the primary law-maker. Legislators are, of course, politicians with party loyalties. When considering the distribution of power between the branches, it is important to remember that the separation of powers is not definitive. Even in the US, with a relatively rigid separation of powers, party priorities can dull the check one branch exerts on the other. In Ireland and the UK, the executive branch – in the form of each country's Cabinet – drives the legislative agenda and drafts the majority of legislative proposals based on promises contained in party platforms.[2] While debate still occurs, it is swift, and is often further circumscribed in more sensitive areas of policy – including where an issue is designated as falling under the category of 'national security'. Where amendments are made through the formal process of debate, they tend to be minor.

While 'disciplining rules' – designed to 'constrain the interpreter and constitute the standards by which the correctness of the interpretation is to be judged' – are essential in legal interpretation, some intentional ambiguity

1　Karen Gebbia-Pinetti, 'Statutory Interpretation, Democratic Legitimacy and Legal-System Values' (1997) 21 *Seton Hall Legislative Journal* 233, 265.
2　It should be noted that the Irish Oireachtas is currently operating in relatively unusual conditions with a minority government supported by a 'confidence and supply' agreement. Under such an arrangement, Private Members Bills are more common although with the resources of the civil service at its behest, the government still adopts a leading role. Fiach Kelly, 'The Full Document: Fine Gael-Fianna Fáil Deal for Government' *The Irish Times* (Dublin, 3 May 2016) <www.irishtimes.com/news/politics/the-full-document-fine-gael-fianna-fáil-deal-for-government-1.2633572>

has attractions for the legislator politician.[3] While some ambiguous terms may be used unintentionally, it is recognised that legislators may at times deliberately make 'use of ambiguities in existing language conventions to further contested political ends'.[4] The motivation for such ambiguities may be to 'make different claims to different constituents or supporters'[5] or to 'purposefully establish the grounds for future debate and disputation'.[6] Ambiguity can also enable legislative compromise and lessen the potential for political cost. As Grundfest and Pritchard argue:

> When legislators perceive a need to compromise they can, among other strategies, 'obscur[e] the particular meaning of a statute, allowing different legislators to read the obscured provisions the way they wish'. Legislative ambiguity reaches its peak when a statute is so elegantly crafted that it credibly supports multiple inconsistent interpretations by legislators and judges. Legislators with opposing views can then claim that they have prevailed in the legislative arena, and, as long as courts continue to issue conflicting interpretations, these competing claims of legislative victory remain credible.[7]

While these strategies may have some utility for the legislator, the legislative ambiguity will result in legal uncertainty and increase the likelihood of a need for judicial determination. This is, of course, not ideal in any context, but it is particularly problematic in the surveillance context where an ambiguity is unlikely to be discovered and is even less likely to ever face a meaningful challenge.

While absolute certainty is unlikely to ever be achieved in human language,[8] technical subjects create additional challenges for legislators. While legislators

3 Dennis Patterson, 'Interpretation in Law – Toward a Reconstruction of the Current Debate' (1984) 29 *Villanova Law Review* 671, 678; Owen Fiss, 'Objectivity and Interpretation' (1982) 34(4) *Stanford Law Review* 739, 744.
4 Ian Bartrum, 'Wittgenstein's Poker: Contested Constitutionalism and the Limits of Public Meaning Originalism' (2017) 10 *Washington University Jurisprudence Review* 29, 32.
5 Saul Levmore, 'Ambiguous Statutes' (2009) 77(4) *University of Chicago Law Review* 8.
6 Ian Bartrum, 'Wittgenstein's Poker: Contested Constitutionalism and the Limits of Public Meaning Originalism' (2017) 10 *Washington University Jurisprudence Review* 29, 51.
7 Joseph Grundfest and Adam Pritchard, 'Statutes with Multiple Personality Disorders: The Value of Ambiguity in Statutory Design and Interpretation' (2002) 54(4) *Stanford Law Review* 627, 628, quoting Abner Mikva and Eric Lane, *An Introduction to Statutory Interpretation and Legislative Process* (Aspen Publishers 1997) 779–780.
8 As Karl Llewellyn suggested: 'Every single precedent, according to what may be the attitude of future judges, is ambiguous'. Karl Llewellyn, *The Bramble Bush: On Our Law and its Study* (Oceana 1951) 71.

are generalists by their nature, nuanced distinctions of language can be the difference between a piece of legislation achieving its intended purpose and not causing unintended deleterious consequences. Challenges are posed when technical language is required to communicate the core meaning of a law – consider the task of regulating complex financial models. If knowing the meaning of a word is knowing 'how that word functions in a discourse', one can see how the disconnect between the politicians passing laws and the members of the executive executing the laws on the ground can lead to surveillance laws being applied in unexpected ways.[9] There is a gap in understanding between those fluent in technical language and those not and, indeed, between those who wilfully misinterpret or under-interpret for political gain. If the true meaning of a law (as applied) only becomes apparent after the law has begun to be used for surveillance, an absence of accountability and review undermines the legitimacy of any claim to foreseeability. Where significant swathes of the community do not merely struggle to understand the terminology – but to understand the underlying concepts and mechanisms of a law – the ability to derive common meaning across relevant groups is threatened. Technology companies may interpret their technical capabilities to be exhausted at a particular point, citizens may accept the glossed over-simplification of their public representative, and investigative authorities – guided by their own particular perspectives and motivations – tend to exert the most control over what interpretation stands in practice.

The folly of 'future proofing' and technology neutrality

A metaphor that appears ever-pervasive in discussions of technology regulation is the metaphor of the law being in a race with technology. In this depiction, the law is always lagging behind the swift progress of technological development. Law is represented as a slow-moving force, almost immediately anachronistic when drafted with specificity. The need to update the law in response to technological advances is viewed as inefficient and so the goal shifts to legislators attempting to 'future proof' their legislation. While all legislatures aim to 'future proof' their legislation to some extent, and a degree of prediction will almost always be involved, the abdication of future responsibility for regulating an area are quite notable when regulating technology. The fact that such drafting often tends to have a bias towards permissive use of new technologies raises particular issues when future developments have human rights implications.

---

9   Christopher Stone, 'From a Language Perspective' (1981) 90(5) *Yale Law Journal* 1149, 1158; Dennis Patterson, 'Interpretation in Law – Toward a Reconstruction of the Current Debate' (1984) 29(621) *Villanova Law Review* 681.

As surveillance laws inevitably involve the use of technology, an early drafting question that must be addressed by legislators is whether to legislate in a technology neutral or technology specific manner. Technology neutrality has been accepted by many as the preferable means by which to regulate. Instead of focusing on the technology itself, technology neutral laws set out to regulate the effects of the relevant technology. The 'lodestar' for technology neutrality is 'intent to regulate behavior, not technology; to worry about what occurs, not how it occurs'.[10] Accordingly, technology neutral laws 'should refer to the effects, functions, or general characteristics of technology, but never to a particular type or class of technology'.[11] In recent decades, there has been an increased adoption of technology neutral laws – including in the surveillance context.[12] The push for such regulation is driven by a number of arguments. The most frequent case made in favour of technology neutral laws in the surveillance context is that surveillance powers should not be restricted based on arbitrary technological distinctions. As adopting a technology neutral approach in surveillance legislation effectively grants greater power to the executive branch, it is unsurprising that representatives of the intelligence community are widely in favour of technology neutral laws. When pressing for a technology neutral approach, representatives of the intelligence community often make the 'common sense' case, pointing out how the deliberative process of the legislative branch fails to keep pace in the fast-paced world of communications technology, while also alluding to their executive competence and expertise. Testifying before Congress the Former Director of National Intelligence, Michael McConnell, stated that

[o]ur job is to make the country as safe as possible by providing the highest quality intelligence available. There is no reason to tie the Nation's security to a snapshot of outdated technology.[13]

---

10 Brad Greenberg, 'Rethinking Technology Neutrality' (2016) 100 *Minnesota Law Review* 1495, 1512.
11 Paul Ohm, 'The Argument against Technology-Neutral Surveillance Laws' (2010) 88 *Texas Law Review* 1685.
12 For example, the USA PATRIOT Act and the Protect America Act brought neutrality to various surveillance laws. Yoo and Posner are in favour of this development, praising the USA PATRIOT Act for making FISA warrants technology neutral and thus allowing the 'continuing surveillance of a terrorist target even if he switches communication devices and methods', John Yoo and Eric Posner, 'The Patriot Act Under Fire' *The Wall Street Journal* (New York, 9 December 2003) <www.wsj.com/articles/SB107093402929348400>. Yoo and Posner describe technology neutrality as a 'common-sense adjustment'; Paul Ohm, 'The Argument against Technology-Neutral Surveillance Laws' (2010) 88 *Texas Law Review* 1685, 1690.
13 Paul Ohm, 'The Argument against Technology-Neutral Surveillance Laws' (2010) 88 *Texas Law Review* 1685, 1690.

Depicting the relationship between law and technology in this way supports the reasoning that technology neutral laws are sensible. Yet, technology neutrality is not a 'principle' worthy of protection on its own merits.[14] In fact, specific laws are needed in order to fulfil the rule of law principles and fundamental rights that are an essential element of a modern liberal democracy. While the Fourth Amendment was initially interpreted as a technology specific protection, the US courts recognised that the Amendment was designed to protect 'people not places'. International human rights – like Article 12 ICCPR and Article 8 ECHR – are technology neutral by design. These rights were not created in a vacuum. The importance of choice of language for the distribution of power is evident in the popularity of adopting the deceptively nonthreatening concept of a 'technology neutral' approach to surveillance law drafting.[15] The broadening of existing surveillance powers to apply to new technologies is often characterised as nothing more than a simple format update necessary to 'to maintain the status quo'.[16] In Chapter 2, it was clear that the application of standards developed in a different technological context can have significant implications for the protection of rights in the present.[17]

Adopting technology neutrality as a policy or guiding principle in the surveillance context can amount to an abdication of responsibility on behalf of the legislative branch in favour of the executive branch. If surveillance laws are drafted in technology neutral terms, there is less of a need for the executive branch to consult with the legislative branch. This not only circumscribes the check of the legislature, but also reduces transparency for the public, as the executive branch tends to operate in comparative obscurity in comparison to the legislative branch. This effect is, of course, magnified in the

---

14 Paul Ohm, 'The Argument against Technology-Neutral Surveillance Laws' (2010) 88 *Texas Law Review* 1685; Brad Greenberg, 'Rethinking Technology Neutrality' (2016) 100 *Minnesota Law Review* 1495, 1498.

15 In oral testimony before the Home Affairs Committee, Sir David Omand stated that when the Regulation of Investigatory Powers Bill was being formulated,

> [t]he instructions to parliamentary draftsmen were to make it technology-neutral, because everyone could see that the technology was moving very fast. Parliamentary draftsmen did an excellent job in doing that, but as a result I do not think the ordinary person or Member of Parliament would be able to follow the Act without a lawyer to explain how these different sections interact.
>
> HC Deb 11 February 2014, vol 231

16 Alberto Escudero-Pascual and Ian Hosein, 'Questioning Lawful Access to Traffic Data' (2004) 47(3) *Communications of The Association of Computing Machinery* 78.

17 Chapter 2.

surveillance context. The focus on technology neutrality means that intrusive powers apply regardless of developing privacy risks – 'where the technology goes, so the powers automatically follow'.[18] While many would argue that this is positive – indeed the aim of technology neutral legislation – it ignores the reality that such future proofing pre-empts policy debate and consideration of new privacy harms. As pointed out by Escudero-Pascual and Hosein:

> Traditional investigative powers of access to traffic data were established with traditional technological environments in mind. Governments are now updating these policies to apply to modern communications infrastructures. If governments insist on applying traditional powers to these new infrastructures, the new policies must acknowledge that the data being collected now is separate from tradition.[19]

In light of the already discussed culture of secrecy in the surveillance context, it seems to be particularly important to have effective democratic debate over new surveillance measures. It has been argued that a benefit of technology specific laws is that they can operate as a type of 'technology sunset, expiring not on some arbitrarily defined timetable, but whenever the circumstances demand'.[20] While this might be deemed inefficient by those with absolute trust in the executive branch, the reality is that developments in surveillance technologies often result in new potential privacy harms as well.

Moreover, the degree of abstraction required in order to draft technology neutral laws can raise additional challenges of understanding for the public and indeed the politician asked to vote upon a measure. The open textured nature of technology neutral legislation in a highly technical area like surveillance law leads to legislation that is difficult to penetrate even for those who are engaged in the area. As pointed out by Omand, the technology neutral manner in which the now partially repealed Regulation of Investigatory Powers Act 2000 was drafted meant that the 'the ordinary person or Member of Parliament' would be unable 'to follow the Act without a lawyer'.[21]

18 Graham Smith, 'Future-proofing the Investigatory Powers Bill' (*Cyberleagle*, 15 April 2016) <www.cyberleagle.com/2016/04/future-proofing-investigatory-powers.htm>
19 Alberto Escudero-Pascual and Ian Hosein, 'Questioning Lawful Access to Traffic Data' (2004) 47(3) *Communications of The Association of Computing Machinery* 78.
20 Paul Ohm, 'The Argument against Technology-Neutral Surveillance Laws' (2010) 88 *Texas Law Review* 1685, 1686.
21 HC Deb 11 February 2014, vol 231, 89 <https://publications.parliament.uk/pa/cm201314/cmselect/cmhaff/231/140211.htm>; Graham Smith, 'Future-proofing the Investigatory

In the House of Lords, the Earl of Northesk indicated his dissatisfaction by stating that

> One of the many difficulties I have with the Bill is that, in its strident efforts to be technology neutral, it often conveys the impression that either it is ignorant of the way in which current technology operates, or pretends that there is no technology at all.[22]

Even though the Investigatory Powers Act was introduced containing much detail and providing unprecedented insight into the activities of UK surveillance agencies, it appears that commitment to the principle of 'future proofed' legislation persists.[23] In his report of the Bulk Powers Review, the then Independent Reviewer of Terrorism Legislation, David Anderson stated that:

> Technology and terminology will inevitably change faster than the ability of legislators to keep up. The scheme of the Bill, which it is not my business to disrupt, is of broad future-proofed powers, detailed codes of practice and strong and vigorous safeguards. If the new law is to have any hope of accommodating the evolution of technology over the next 10 or 15 years, it needs to avoid the trap of an excessively prescriptive and technically defined approach.[24]

The House of Commons Science and Technology Committee criticised the attempt to 'future proof' the IPA, arguing that technology neutral and flexible terms such as 'communications content' and 'equipment interference' cause 'significant confusion on the part of communications service providers and others'.[25] The technical nature of the subject matter is not an

---

Powers Bill' (*Cyberleagle*, 15 April 2016) <www.cyberleagle.com/2016/04/future-proofing-investigatory-powers.htm>

22 HL Deb, 28 June 2000, XOL 1012; Alberto Escudero-Pascual and Ian Hosein, 'Questioning Lawful Access to Traffic Data' (2004) 47(3) *Communications of The Association of Computing Machinery* 78.

23 Graham Smith, 'Future-proofing the Investigatory Powers Bill' (*Cyberleagle*, 15 April 2016) <www.cyberleagle.com/2016/04/future-proofing-investigatory-powers.htm>

24 David Anderson, Report of the Bulk Powers Review (Cm 9326, 2016) <https://terrorismlegislationreviewer.independent.gov.uk/wp-content/uploads/2016/08/Bulk-Powers-Review-final-report.pdf>

25 Investigatory Powers Bill: Government Response to Pre-Legislative Scrutiny Presented to Parliament by the Secretary of State for the Home Department by Command of Her Majesty (Cm 9219).

'excuse for obscurity' and clarity for all stakeholders – most importantly for the individual – must be provided.[26]

The Public Services Card in Ireland: 'mandatory' not 'compulsory'

At earlier points in this book, the practice of misrepresenting the privacy implications of a new surveillance practice or technology by downplaying its significance for privacy and taking advantage of the limited technical literacy of the average citizen has been discussed.[27] The roll-out of the Public Services Card (PSC) in Ireland provides an ideal example of political double-speak and technical obfuscation in support of a surveillance system. While the PSC scheme could have been used to illustrate points made in earlier chapters – notably on matters of executive interpretation in Chapter 3 – the PSC debate is discussed here as it draws together several strings of the argument regarding the relationship between the legislative and executive branch in the surveillance sphere. Crucially, the PSC saga illustrates the importance of placing careful limits on executive action through clear and specific laws debated and passed by the legislative branch. When the misleading statements of politicians in defence of the PSC scheme, the claims of 'nothing to see here', and the shaky legal basis are considered as a piece, the dangers of legislating in a haphazard manner in technical areas of pertinence to human rights are starkly apparent. While much of what has been discussed thus far in this book has concerned covert surveillance, the fact that similar tactics are used in an apparently non-covert surveillance context is not surprising considering how the technological comprehension (and attention) gap can facilitate the quiet accretion of authority. It seems clear, however, that recent events demonstrate a need to better communicate the practical effects of surveillance laws to the public, to politicians, and to the broader class of policy-maker – including civil servants.

While Ireland – like the UK and the United States – does not have a tradition of compulsory identity cards, steps towards the introduction of a public services identity card began over a decade ago.[28] Nomenclature has been a

---

26 David Anderson, 'The Investigatory Powers Review: A Question of Trust' (2015) 4 *European Human Rights Law Review* 331.

27 See, for example, Chapter 1.

28 Carl O'Brien, '25m to be Spent on New Public Services ID Cards for Over-16s' *The Irish Times* (Dublin, 31 December 2009) <www.irishtimes.com/news/25m-to-be-spent-on-new-public-services-id-cards-for-over-16s-1.796451>; David Quinn, 'All-in-one Public

key part of the debate, with government representatives repeatedly rejecting the toxic label of 'identity card'. The stated reason for the PSC scheme was the modernisation of public service delivery through the standardisation of identification and authentication procedures across all government agencies. Identified aims of the scheme are increased efficiency and reduced fraud.[29] A key element of the communications strategy has been an insistence that the PSC is a benefit to citizens, widely demanded, and in all cases optional.[30] For example, in August 2017, the Taoiseach stated that

> it is not a national ID card (. . .) the characteristic of a national ID card is that the police or the army can ask you to produce it, that you use it for travel, that's not going to be the case.[31]

This attempt to set the boundaries of legitimate concern is particularly interesting in light of the fact that at the time of the Taoiseach's statement, the government's policy was to make the obtaining of a first passport or driver licence contingent on possession of PSC.[32] Focusing on the semantics of what constitutes an identity card could also be viewed as an act of deflection. The defence that no police officer can ask an individual to 'show me your papers' is underwhelming in light of the essential services effectively closed off to those who resist registering for the scheme. The comment made by the Minister for Employment Affairs and Social Protection, Regina

Service Card Proposed' *Irish Independent* (Dublin, 1 July 2004) <www.independent.ie/irish-news/allinone-public-service-card-proposed-25904454.html>; Office of the Comptroller and Auditor General, Report on the Account of the Public Services (September 2016) 11 <www.audgen.gov.ie/documents/annualreports/2016/report/en/Report_Accounts_Public_Services_2016.pdf>

29 Office of the Comptroller and Auditor General, Report on the Account of the Public Services (September 2016) 11 <www.audgen.gov.ie/documents/annualreports/2016/report/en/Report_Accounts_Public_Services_2016.pdf>

30 Mark Hilliard, 'Public Service Card Use Not Mandatory, says Donohoe' *The Irish Times* (Dublin, 23 March 2017) <www.irishtimes.com/business/technology/public-service-card-use-not-mandatory-says-donohoe-1.3022649>

31 'Taoiseach says Public Services Card not a National ID card' *RTE News* (Dublin, 31 August 2017) <www.rte.ie/news/ireland/2017/0831/901203-public-services-card/>

32 Daragh Brophy, 'You'll Soon Need a Public Services Card to Renew your Passport' *The Journal* (Dublin, 28 August 2017/) <www.thejournal.ie/public-services-card-passports-3568044-Aug2017/>; Cianan Brennan, 'You're Going to Need a PSC to get any Kind of Driving Licence or Learner Permit from April' *The Journal* (Dublin, 20 February 2018) <www.thejournal.ie/psc-driving-licences-3861387-Feb2018/>; but see Cianan Brennan, 'It Turns out you WON'T need a PSC to apply for your Driving Licence after all' *The Journal* (Dublin, 27 March 2018) <www.thejournal.ie/psc-driving-licence-3926469-Mar2018/>

Doherty, that it would be 'mandatory' but not 'compulsory' to register for the PSC in order to access essential social benefits – including pensions and children's allowance – illustrates the fallacious position adopted on the topic when confronted with a concerned public.[33] Tying essential benefits and state services to a person's compliance with the new regime certainly fails to meet the understanding of consent under European Union data protection law and the Minister for Social Protection's assertion that '[n]obody will drag you kicking and screaming' does little to reassure of the genuineness of citizen choice.[34]

Another example of how the government has distorted language in the debate on this topic in order to defend the PSC programme is provided by its contestation over the meaning of the term 'biometric'. Government representatives have consistently rejected claims that the PSC scheme collects and stores biometric data.[35] The fact that the scheme collects facial images that can be used to run facial recognition processes is dismissed by the government as simply the taking of 'photographs'. As discussed previously, where technical language is involved, there is scope to mislead. In May 2018, Minister Doherty responded to a Parliamentary Question with the statement that:

> We do not collect biometric data. We collect and store photographs. If someone has a public services card, they come in and get their photograph taken, we store that photograph and it gets put on the person's card. It is as benign as that.[36]

33 Niall O'Connor, 'Row as Minister Says Public Services Card "Mandatory but not Compulsory"' *Irish Independent* (Dublin, 26 August 2017) <www.independent.ie/irish-news/politics/row-as-minister-says-public-services-card-mandatory-but-not-compulsory-36070692.html>

34 Michael Staines, 'Minister says Public Services Card "Mandatory" but not "Compulsory"' *NewsTalk* (Dublin, 25 August 2017) <www.newstalk.com/Minister-says-Public-Services-Card-mandatory-but-not-compulsory>. The reporting on the story of a pensioner who chose not to register for the system and accordingly had her pension denied for over a year brought significant additional attention to the issue in August 2017: Elaine Edwards, 'Woman's Pension Cut After She Refuses to get Public Services Card' *The Irish Times* (Dublin, 22 August 2017) <www.irishtimes.com/news/social-affairs/woman-s-pension-cut-after-she-refuses-to-get-public-services-card-1.3194216>

35 See the numerous tweets by the Minister for Social Protection, Regina Doherty, as archived on the Privacy Kit Website Public Services Card media coverage web page <myprivacykit.com/public-services-card-media-coverage/>

36 Question by Catherine Murphy to Minister for Employment Affairs and Social Protection, Departmental Records Dáil Éireann Debate (3 May 2018) <www.oireachtas.ie/index.php/en/debates/question/2018-05-03/5/?highlight%5B0%5D=catherine&highlight%5B1%5D=murphy&highlight%5B2%5D=biometric#pq-answers>

This statement attempts to normalise the process, but also misleads through its very specific choice of words. According to the Minister, the Department of Social Protection uses facial image matching software in order to ensure that individuals cannot register for the PSC under a different Personal Public Service Number or a different identity dataset. In order to do this facial matching, the Department uses software that compares photographs by converting images into arithmetic templates based on facial characteristics and checking those templates against image templates already stored.[37] The Minister's assertion that 'we are not considering a photograph as biometric data. It is just a photograph' does not engage with the legal reality that biometric data includes any

> personal data resulting from specific technical processing relating to the physical, physiological or behavioural characteristics of a natural person, which allow or confirm the unique identification of that natural person, such as facial images.[38]

The implementation of the PSC and its associated identity index database has clear implications for human rights – most obviously the rights to privacy and the protection of personal data. The physical card is not where the primary privacy threat rests, but in the collection and processing of data. As pointed out by Digital Rights Ireland,

> [t]he Public Services Card is actually much bigger than the card itself. It is a plan that will result in the linking up of private, intimate details of Irish citizens' lives across all sections of government, including the education system, Gardaí and the Health Service.[39]

It is recognised that the processing of information relating to an individual's private life falls within the scope of Article 8 ECHR.[40] Even 'public information can fall within the scope of private life where it is systematically collected and stored in files' held by government.[41] In addition to the right to respect for private life as found in the European Convention on Human Rights, Articles 7 and 8 of the Charter of Fundamental Rights

---

37 Question by Clare Daly to Minister for Employment Affairs and Social Protection, Public Services Card Data Dáil Éireann Debate (3 May 2018) <www.oireachtas.ie/en/debates/debate/dail/2018-06-19/478/>
38 General Data Protection Regulation, art 4(14).
39 Digital Rights Ireland, 'New "Egovernment" Strategy is a National Identity Card by the Back Door' (*Digital Rights Ireland*, 2 August 2017) <www.digitalrights.ie/new-egovernment-strategy/>
40 See, for example, *Rotaru v Romania* [2000] ECHR 192.
41 *Rotaru v Romania* [2000] ECHR 192.

of the European Union are also clearly relevant. As has been discussed throughout this book, any intrusion with a fundamental right should have a clear legal basis.[42] In fact, the existence of a legal basis is the most basic aspect of the legality test. Subsequent to extensive case law on the point, governments often pass this first legality hurdle with ease. This should be particularly straightforward where the surveillance measure in issue is not a covert measure as there would appear to be no operational secrecy imperative. In spite of this, the legal basis for the PSC is highly contested. It has been remarked by many that the claimed legal basis for the PSC and the related 'Public Services Identity' is unhelpfully disparate and difficult to follow.[43] The legal basis the Department of Social Protection has relied upon to deny benefits to individuals who have not registered for the PSC is the Social Welfare Consolidation Act 2005, as amended by the Social Welfare and Pensions (Miscellaneous Provisions) Act 2013. Under Section 247C(1) of the 2005 Act, the Minister 'may give notice to any person receiving a benefit' requesting that the person, 'at the time specified in the notice, to satisfy the Minister as to his or her identity'. Section 247C(2) of the Act provides that a person who fails to satisfy the Minister in relation to their identity may be disqualified from receiving the relevant benefit. Section 247C(3) of the Act sets out the process by which a person's identity can be 'authenticated'.[44] The person may, 'for the purposes of the authentication' be required to provide 'any document to the Minister as the Minister may reasonably require'; 'allow a photograph or other record' of their image to be taken; and/or provide a sample of his or her signature in electronic form. As pointed out by McGarr, section 247C(3) does not state that the purpose of this process 'is to have your data entered onto the national Public Services Card register or the Single Customer View database, with all the subsequent data sharing and processing that involves'.[45] In fact, the Act explicitly states

42 See, in particular, Chapter 3.
43 'Is the Public Services Card Mandatory to Access State Services?' (*Digital Rights Ireland*, 29 August 2017) <www.digitalrights.ie/public-services-card-mandatory-access-state-services/>
44 Simon McGarr, 'The Public Services Card: Mandatory, Without a Mandate' (8 February 2018) Oireachtas Submission on Public Services Card 4 <https://data.oireachtas.ie/ie/oireachtas/committee/dail/32/joint_committee_on_employment_affairs_and_social_protection/submissions/2018/2018-02-08_opening-statement-simon-mcgarr-mcgarr-solicitors_en.pdf>
45 Simon McGarr, 'The Public Services Card: Mandatory, Without a Mandate' (8 February 2018) Oireachtas Submission on Public Services Card 5 <https://data.oireachtas.ie/ie/oireachtas/committee/dail/32/joint_committee_on_employment_affairs_and_social_protection/submissions/2018/2018-02-08_opening-statement-simon-mcgarr-mcgarr-solicitors_en.pdf>

that the records generated by this attendance should only be used 'to satisfy the Minister as to his or her identity'.[46] Accordingly, it would appear
to be outside the scope of that legal authority to engage in further use of
the collected data.[47] While section 247C(2) provides that an individual's
benefit can be denied where their identity has not been authenticated, this
section has been relied upon to deny benefits to individuals who have
demonstrated their identity by other means – including by the provision
of passports and utility bills.

In the 2016 Annual Report of the Irish data protection authority, the Data
Protection Commissioner (DPC), it was stated that the

> implementation of large-scale government projects without specific
> legislative underpinning, but rather relying on generic provisions in
> various pieces of legislation, poses challenges in terms of the transpar-
> ency to the public.[48]

In August 2017, the DPC stated that 'there is a pressing need for updated,
clearer and more detailed information to be communicated to the public and
services users regarding the mandatory use of the Public Services Card for
accessing public services'.[49] Similar to the manner in which the challenges
of technical understanding can allow for the obfuscation of surveillance
measures from the public, complex legal arguments can achieve similar
effects. The PSC debate has seen evidence of both tactics. While strong
points have been made to discredit the claimed legal basis for the expanded
use of the PSC, and in spite of an ongoing investigation by the DPC, government representatives have been most confident in asserting that a lawful

46 Simon McGarr, 'The Public Services Card: Mandatory, Without a Mandate' (8 February 2018) Oireachtas Submission on Public Services Card 5 <https://data.oireachtas.ie/
   ie/oireachtas/committee/dail/32/joint_committee_on_employment_affairs_and_social_
   protection/submissions/2018/2018-02-08_opening-statement-simon-mcgarr-mcgarr-solici
   tors_en.pdf>
47 Simon McGarr, 'The Public Services Card: Mandatory, Without a Mandate' (8 February 2018) Oireachtas Submission on Public Services Card 5 <https://data.oireachtas.ie/
   ie/oireachtas/committee/dail/32/joint_committee_on_employment_affairs_and_social_
   protection/submissions/2018/2018-02-08_opening-statement-simon-mcgarr-mcgarr-solici
   tors_en.pdf>
48 2016 Annual Report of the Data Protection Commissioner of Ireland Presented to each of
   the Houses of the Oireachtas, pursuant to Section 14 of the Data Protection Acts 1988 and
   2003 <www.dataprotection.ie/documents/annualreports/AnnualReport16.pdf>
49 Data Protection Commissioner Statement on the Public Services Card (dataprotection.
   ie: 30 August 2017) <www.dataprotection.ie/docs/EN/30-08-2017-Data-Protection-Com
   misisoners-Statement-on-the-Public-Services-Card/b/1651.htm>

basis does indeed exist.[50] The Minister for Finance & Public Expenditure and Reform, Pascal Donohoe, maintains that the 'development of the card and the associated legislation has happened in a completely democratic and transparent way'.[51] The official position regarding the PSC has consistently been that it is a positive measure that the people are demanding. If the PSC is indeed such a popular measure with the general population as is claimed, it would seem logical that clear legislation providing for the scheme would be a positive political gain for the initiating government. Yet, the legal basis remains uncertain.

Legislative abdication

In a similar manner to how technology neutral laws allow for expansion of authority with lessened scrutiny, the lack of insistence on specific and clear laws can also lead to function creep and bureaucratic expansion of intrusive policies without adequate consideration of rights. In addition to the requirements of accessibility and foreseeability in a democratic society, another crucial function of clear legislation is to adequately circumscribe the role of the executive. Where the legislative branch fails to provide a clear and specific legal basis for executive action, an opportunity for function creep will arise. In an email (obtained via a Freedom of Information Request) from the DPC to the Department of Social Protection in August 2016, the DPC warned that

> as a risk of functional creep, intentionally or otherwise, there is a risk that the PSC will be altered from one which contains limited information existing to facilitate transactions with public services into a form of national ID card.[52]

---

50 Although the recent distancing efforts by the Department of Transport are noteworthy: Cianan Brennan, '"The Deeper I Go, the more Concern I have" – Department of Transport Worried over "Exposure" due to Mandatory PSC' *The Journal* (Dublin, 5 June 2018) <www.thejournal.ie/department-transport-psc-foi-4048883-Jun2018/>

51 In correspondence with the Irish Council of Civil Liberties. Elaine Edwards, '"Massive Privacy Issues" in State's Public Services Card Scheme' *The Irish Times* (Dublin, 11 October 2017) <www.irishtimes.com/news/social-affairs/massive-privacy-issues-in-state-s-public-services-card-scheme-1.3252742>

52 Elaine Edwards, 'Commissioner Feared Potential for form of National ID Card' *The Irish Times* (Dublin, 5 September 2017) <www.irishtimes.com/news/social-affairs/commissioner-feared-potential-for-form-of-national-id-card-1.3210594>

Function creep is not unusual in this area. In India, the controversial Aadhaar project shifted from a voluntary scheme to being mandatory for obtaining state services, including for paying taxes and for opening a bank account. Where legitimate complaints are deflected and dismissed, and where the legislative branch appears to place little effective constraint on executive action, the necessity of an additional check on executive power becomes clear. When the reaction to public and expert concern is not to consider the legal basis or indeed the proportionality of a project, but to fund a promotional campaign touting its benefits, a degree of accountability appears to be lacking.[53] The likelihood of this type of situation arising in Ireland would appear to be increased by the fused system of governance where the Cabinet is comprised of senior members of the majority party or coalition parties. While it is notable that the sequence of events discussed above have primarily taken place under the unusual arrangement of a minority government supported by a 'confidence and supply' agreement, similar dynamics have been evident.[54] Where the executive appears to be acting outside of the scope of its legislative-granted authority, an interested party may seek a determination from the judicial branch. Accordingly, it seems likely that litigation will be required in order to determine the true legal status of the PSC.

53 Elaine Edwards, 'Government Plans €200,000 Public Services Card Campaign' *The Irish Times* (Dublin, 22 October 2017) <www.irishtimes.com/news/ireland/irish-news/government-plans-200-000-public-services-card-campaign-1.3265101>
54 Fiach Kelly, 'The Full Document: Fine Gael-Fianna Fáil Deal for Government' *The Irish Times* (Dublin, 3 May 2016) <www.irishtimes.com/news/politics/the-full-document-fine-gael-fianna-fáil-deal-for-government-1.2633572>

Conclusion

Following its review of US domestic surveillance practices in 1976 – a review initially sparked by the theft of classified documents subsequently shared with media outlets[1] – the Church Committee concluded that the 'system of checks and balances' had not adequately controlled intelligence activities.[2] In light of the discussion of technological evolution in this book, it is also notable that it was already being remarked in the 1970s that the 'rapid development of technology in the area of electronic surveillance has seriously aggravated present ambiguities in the law'.[3] In response to the findings of the Church Committee, legislative reforms were introduced to provide greater transparency of US surveillance practices and to require additional oversight of the intelligence agencies by both Congress and the courts. The Snowden revelations – which uncovered a remarkable discrepancy between government surveillance practice and rule of law standards – exposed how these considered remedies had been eroded over time. This should serve as a caution that constant vigilance is required if power is not to be abused.

While this book considered the importance of the different branches of government placing checks on government authority, the case studies demonstrated how the legislative and judicial branches often fail to provide a meaningful check on executive power and acquiesce to assertions of competence. In 1980, Donner wrote that '[a]ll wars glamorize and popularize intelligence and at the same time release into a postwar society cadres

1 Betty Medsger, *The Burglary: The Discovery of J Edgar Hoover's Secret FBI* (Alfred Knopf 2014).
2 Intelligence Activities and the Rights of Americans, Final Report of the Senate Select Committee to Study Governmental Operations with Respect to Intelligence Activities (1976) S Rep No 94-755, Book ii.
3 Intelligence Activities: Hearing on S Res 21 Before the Select Committee to Study Governmental Operations with Respect to Intelligence Activities of the United States (1975) 65.

trained in intelligence practice'.[4] In the perpetual state of war that is being waged, at least in the rhetorical sense,[5] the post-war cadres 'trained in intelligence practices' have been replaced by the surveillance industrial complex that profits from surveillance and employs – and contracts – an enormous number of surveillance professionals.[6] While the political heads of the executive branch possess the constitutional powers and are subject to electoral censure, the apparatus of national security – of which surveillance is an ever-increasing part – has been 'colonized by a new nobility of intelligence agencies operating in an increasingly autonomous transnational arena'.[7] There is a pressing risk that the concentration of 'secret power in the hands of intelligence agencies may prove deeply corrosive to democracy, commerce, and the rule of law'.[8] Accordingly, it is necessary to consider how adequate transparency can be provided in order to keep the actions of government authorities under appropriate democratic review.

It has been shown how choice and interpretation of language can have far reaching effects when drafting legislation[9] and internal executive guidelines;[10] when interpreting constitutional principles in light of the modern context;[11] when applying laws on the ground;[12] and when advocating for a new policy in the political sphere.[13] This book has illustrated how attention to language choice and use is particularly important in the surveillance sphere where terms have been interpreted in ways divergent from their generally understood meanings,[14] where technological realities have been ignored,[15] and where technological misunderstandings have been exploited.[16] The complexities of the technologies central to modern surveillance –

4 Frank Donner, *The Age of Surveillance: The Aims and Methods of America's Political Intelligence System* (Vintage Books 1980) 25.
5 Brian Michael Jenkins, 'Fifteen Years On, Where are we in the "War on Terror"?' (2016) 9(9) *CTC Sentinel* 7.
6 Kirstie Ball and Laureen Snider (eds), *The Surveillance Industrial Complex: Towards a Political Economy of Surveillance* (Routledge 2013).
7 Zygmunt Bauman, Didier Bigo, Paulo Esteves, Elspeth Guild, Vivienne Jabri, David Lyon, and Rob Walker, 'After Snowden: Rethinking the Impact of Surveillance' (2014) 8 *International Political Sociology* 121, 126.
8 Douwe Korff, Ben Wagner, Julia Powles, Renata Avila, and Ulf Buermeyer, 'Global Report – Boundaries of Law Exploring Transparency, Accountability, and Oversight of Government Surveillance Regimes' (January 2017) 11.
9 Chapter 5.
10 Chapter 3.
11 Chapter 2.
12 Chapters 2 and 3.
13 Chapter 1.
14 Chapters 3 and 4.
15 Chapters 1 and 5.
16 Chapters 1, 3, 4, and 5.

and the implications of their exploitation in practical terms – can be difficult to comprehend for the average person. As a result, the parties with power have an opportunity to represent the issue in the way that best serves their purposes. Chapter 1 illustrated how metaphors and over-simplification of the technical challenges have been used to distract from legitimate concerns about the undermining of encryption tools essential for the protection of privacy. Similarly, in Chapter 5, the stealth expansion of the Irish Public Services Card has been accompanied by denials and misdirections by government representatives regarding the technical realities and implications of the scheme. Surveillance law brings together the elements of secrecy, technical complexity, and fear that causes the average citizen to place their trust in the executive branch and its agencies. What is clear, is that left unchecked, that trust is liable for abuse.

As asserted by the Church Committee's domestic task force:

> Knowledge is the key to control. Secrecy should no longer be allowed to shield the existence of the constitutional, legal and moral problems from the scrutiny of government or from the American people themselves.[17]

The existence of 'secret law' in the surveillance context is the most blatant example of a lack of knowledge enabling a culture of impunity. Chapter 3 considered the divergent interpretation of words as generally understood in order to support expansive surveillance programmes. Even though the UK has intermittently legislated to put its surveillance regimes on a clearer legal basis in response to calls for greater accessibility and foreseeability by the European Court of Human Rights, the development of programmes under questionable legal bases prior to the Snowden leaks does not engender confidence in the ability of the Investigatory Powers Act to constrain in the manner attested by its supporters. Beyond the demonstrated difficulty of placing limits on executive action through legislation,[18] it is necessary to consider the safeguard provided by the judiciary. While constitutional and human rights courts have placed limits on surveillance measures, it is judges – or judge-like actors – on the ground that are best placed to identify when surveillance laws are

---

17 Intelligence Activities and the Rights of Americans, Final Report of the Senate Select Committee to Study Governmental Operations with Respect to Intelligence Activities (1976) S Rep No 94-755, Book ii, 292; Walter Mondale, Robert Stein, and Caitlinrose Fisher, 'No Longer a Neutral Magistrate: The Foreign Intelligence Surveillance Court in the Wake of the War on Terror' (2016) 100 *Minnesota Law Review* 2251, 2312.
18 Particularly where the legislature opts to legislate in a technology neutral manner; see Chapter 5.

being interpreted in unforeseen ways. Chapter 3 discussed how in addition to providing judicial legitimacy to executive expansions of surveillance power, the Foreign Intelligence Surveillance Court was regularly stunted in its ability to place meaningful limits on the intelligences agencies with which the agencies would actually comply. In addition to the effect secrecy has on the potency of court decisions, the cloistered and ex parte manner in which surveillance courts tend to operate means that the work of the overseers themselves also often escapes public scrutiny.

In spite of the necessity of openness for the proper operation of the checks and balances of government being identified following the Church Committee investigations, the legislative responses floundered over time. Increased congressional oversight was a key recommendation of the Church Committee, but James Clapper's evasion of Senator Wyden's questions – as discussed in Chapter 3 – rendered the Senator's special knowledge as a member of the Senate Intelligence Committee impotent for the purposes of holding the executive branch to account. Similarly, the manner in which the FISC repeatedly attempted to hold the NSA to account and were met with continual non-compliance, shows how without open justice, the courts are hamstrung in their functions. These examples demonstrate that where transparency is limited to the other branches of government, challenges to constraining the executive branch will persist. As Manes asks, '[m]ust we depend on the happenstance of a public-spirited whistleblower willing to risk years in prison – or exile – to learn how the government understands the laws meant to constrain surveillance?'[19]

It is maintained that the principle of openness, as vaunted by the Church Committee; and the principles of accessibility and foreseeability, as emphasised by the European Court of Human Rights over decades; remain key if the citizenry are to regain control of the issue. If law is not to serve as a loose veil of legitimacy, however, it is essential that society is alive to the possibility that the superficial appearance of protections may not reflect reality. Accordingly, mechanisms that interrogate the practice and not just the promise of the law are of paramount importance. Two notable developments on this point that have emerged following the Snowden revelations are the amendments to the operation of the FISC and the establishment of the Office of the Investigatory Powers Commissioner. A relevant change to FISC processes is the requirement – subject to some exceptions – that the government declassify each decision, order, or opinion issued by the FISC

19 Jonathan Manes, 'Online Service Providers and Surveillance Law Transparency' (2016) 125 *Yale Law Journal Forum* 343, 347.

that includes a significant construction or interpretation of any provision of law, including any novel or significant construction or interpretation of the term 'specific selection term', and, consistent with that review, make publicly available to the greatest extent practicable each such decision, order, or opinion.[20]

As mentioned in Chapter 3, this improvement may still be limited in its effectiveness if key terms – such as 'significant' are interpreted narrowly. A standard in favour of publication would be preferable; and ideally, the assessment should be made by an independent party.[21]

Turning to the IPC and the Judicial Commissioners that were established to provide oversight of UK surveillance practices under the IPA. While Chapter 3 discussed how the 'double-lock' system constitutes judicial 'approval' rather than judicial 'authorisation', the procedure does insert an independent third-party at the ex ante stage of surveillance operations. In principle, this will provide the Judicial Commissioners with insight into how the law is being applied in practice in a vast array of cases. In addition to the IPC's considerable audit, inspection, and investigation duties,[22] the extensive reporting requirements have the potential to make the practical operation of UK surveillance law more transparent.[23] One notable item that the annual report must include is information about the work of the Technology Advisory Panel that is required to provide advice on the 'impact of changing technology on the exercise of investigatory powers'.[24] With the appropriate resourcing and expertise, this function has the potential to address the knowledge inequality that has been exploited by the executive branch in the past. It remains the case, however, that the transparency provided by these powers will depend on the willingness of the IPC to take advantage of the scope provided by the IPA to bring the adopted interpretations and applications to public view.[25]

---

20 The USA Freedom Act, Public Law No 114-23, ss 402 and 602.
21 The USA Freedom Act, Public Law No 114-23, ss 402 and 602.
22 IPA, s 229.
23 Subject to the provision that the exercising of their functions is not 'contrary to the public interest or prejudicial to – (a) national security, (b) the prevention or detection of serious crime, or (c) the economic well-being of the United Kingdom'. IPA, s 229(6); see also IPA, s 229(7).
24 IPA, ss 234(g), 246.
25 Graham Smith, 'The Investigatory Powers Act – Swan or Turkey?' (*Cyberleagle*, 31 December 2016) <www.cyberleagle.com/2016/12/the-investigatory-powers-act-swan-or.html>

While insider revelations, court cases, and Freedom of Information requests have provided greater insight into the activities of intelligence agencies, the reality is that the current operation of intelligence activities remains uncertain. This limits the ability to argue for the appropriate policy response or procedural and institutional reforms with exactitude. Where secrecy exists there will always be the potential for 'the destruction of meaning' and the use and abuse of language will play an essential role in that destruction.[26] In light of history, it is not unreasonable to contemplate whether 'the limits that we think various statutes impose on governmental surveillance prove illusory if the government continues to embroider them with layers of secret meaning?'[27] Establishing safeguards under law will never be a guarantee of effective protection of rights or accountable government. Without such safeguards, however, arbitrary exercise of authority is inevitable. Similarly, perfect transparency is impossible and it will not solve all of the problems of government excess, yet robust mechanisms of transparency are essential in order to place a degree of democratic accountability on those granted such significant power. While the safeguard of the IPC and the amendments to the FISC procedures should provide greater transparency of surveillance powers and engender informed debate on their scope and operation, their effectiveness remains uncertain. It is positive that these new iterations of oversight build in an opportunity for the public to scrutinise the use of powers wielded in their name. It seems certain, however, that further iterations will be necessary when flaws in these systems are identified. It is also without doubt that the watchdog role of the citizen and civil society will continue to be central as any notion of 'trust' must be continually kept under scrutiny.

26 There has been significant discussion in this book about the ambiguity of human language and about how this ambiguity can be exploited by those in power, particularly when the area involves technology. This critique should not be seen as an endorsement of other measures deemed more impartial as it is very clear that seemingly objective facts and figures can also be manipulated to support a particular policy position or legal outcome. Moreover, fealty to the notion that algorithms provide an unbiased alternative is also clearly flawed. For some of the risks of algorithmic surveillance, see Maria Helen Murphy, 'Algorithmic Surveillance: The Collection Conundrum' (2017) 31(2) *International Review of Law, Computers & Technology* 225.

27 Jonathan Manes, 'Online Service Providers and Surveillance Law Transparency' (2016) 125 *Yale Law Journal Forum* 343, 347.

Index